No Time Lost

NO TIME LOST

Walter Mack

With Peter Buckley

New York ATHENEUM 1982

Library of Congress Cataloging in Publication Data
Mack, Walter.
    No time lost.

    1. Pepsi-Cola Company—History. 2. Mack, Walter.
3. Businessmen—United States—Biography. I. Buckley,
Peter. II. Title.
HD9349.S634P465   1982   338.7′66362′0924   [B]   82-71061
ISBN 0-689-11326-9   AACR2

Published simultaneously in Canada by McClelland and Stewart Ltd.
Composed by American–Stratford Graphic Services,
Brattleboro, Vermont
Manufactured by Fairfield Graphics, Fairfield, Pennsylvania
Designed by Mary Cregan
First Edition

Without my wife, R U T H *, always at hand*
to offer support and encouragement,
No Time Lost *would have been much time lost,*
and for that lifetime of sharing
I submit this memoir

Introduction

For years I've been thinking about writing my own story and telling the whole tale, the story I've been living and the tale I've been handing out in bits and pieces over the past sixty-odd years, but somehow I could never get around to it. I'm not much of a writer; I'm not much of a reader; I'm really not even much of a thinker: I'm a doer. But maybe my life has been just a little bit different, a little out of the ordinary. It's certainly been longer than most lives, and as it's rambled along its course it has brought me face to face with some of the best—as well as some of the worst—that this century has had to offer so far.

I am in my eighty-seventh year now, starting up a

Introduction

new multimillion-dollar international company, and as fit and full of fight as ever, but if I don't get my story down now, I may not have another chance. Not that I don't intend to be around a good while longer, but I'm a busy man—I've always been a busy man, which is probably why I am still around—as well as a happy, contented man. I have no ax to grind, no scores to settle, no demons to exorcise, no buried bodies to exhume. But I do have a story to tell, the story of one man in this country in this century.

I was born into an innocent world where all was orderly and genteel, protected from poverty and misery. We grew up in the war years—the First War—and cut our teeth on Prohibition. During the twenties anything was possible and everybody seemed to be in on the game, while during the thirties nothing was supposed to be possible yet we all managed to work minor miracles. We not only survived, we grew, and as we came out of the Depression, I went into my great adventure with Pepsi-Cola. The forties plunged us into a new and even more terrible war, but the postwar years saw the country grow beyond our wildest dreams. Over the last generation our country has gone through a social revolution of sorts, and today we live in an age that is supposed to idealize youth; yet it is an age when a youngster like me can start anew with a company of his own, with an eye on the future. I've grown with this century and with this country, and I've seen changes that no man could have predicted— changes in the world, in my immediate surroundings, and most of all in myself.

I am an unrepentant capitalist and a liberal (the two have always lived comfortably within my personal philosophy), and a political fighter, but other than that I don't think of myself as a particularly unusual man. I'm not all that much smarter than the next fellow, but I have been luckier, that's for sure. So I feel, since my life and times are a minor reflection of this country in this century, that perhaps I should tell a little about myself to anybody who wants to listen.

Contents

I

The Early Years:
My Coming-Out Party
to the World

I

All things considered, 1895 was not such a bad year. Grover Cleveland was in the White House, and it would be another three years before his successor, William McKinley, would be forced to get us involved in the Spanish-American War. Queen Victoria had been on her throne for fifty-eight years, and except for some fleeting skirmishes around her vast empire, the Pax Brittanica was very much in force. And it would be yet another nineteen years before her assorted in-laws became embroiled in a family squabble of sorts that would tear apart the world as it was known at the time.

In Russia, as the pogroms continued and millions

emigrated, Czar Alexander III was making good his promise to kill off a third of his country's Jews, convert another third, and drive out the remainder. Anti-Semitism was on the rise on the Continent, and the trial of one Captain Alfred Dreyfus was a continuing scandal in France. A young Hungarian journalist, Theodor Herzl, had returned to Vienna after covering the Dreyfus case for that city's *Neue Frei Presse* to work out a solution to the Jewish problem in Europe and was laying the foundation of political Zionism.

In America, racial tensions were riding high, lynchings hardly news anymore, and segregation on an "equal but separate" footing was a growing legal way of life in over half our land. The entire country was in the third year of a deep economic depression. The bottom started to drop out of Wall Street in May 1893, and on June 27 the market collapsed. Over the next few months six hundred banks closed their doors, seventy-four railroads bailed out, and over fifteen thousand businesses dried up. That year Kelly's Army of fifteen hundred unemployed marched on Washington demanding jobs that just weren't available. Coxey's Army of four hundred unemployed followed the same route a year later and came away with the same results.

By 1895 things hadn't improved all that much. Wheat prices were down to 49¢ a bushel, less than half of what it had been selling for a decade before, which was a good indicator that there just wasn't enough money to go around. Except, of course, for the few, because there seemed to be millionaires aplenty, especially in New York. In a feeble effort to spread the wealth around a little, the Wilson-Gorman Tariff Act of 1894 called for a 2 percent tax on incomes over

$4,000, but the act was labeled "communistic and so-cialistic," and on May 20, 1895, the Supreme Court ruled it unconstitutional.

Coca-Cola had first been introduced in Atlanta nine years before, and by 1895 its owner, Asa Candler, would boast that it was being sold in every state of the Union, even though it wouldn't be bottled until the end of the century. A pharmacist by the name of Caleb Bradham had been mixing fountain drinks in New Bern, North Carolina, for two years, but it wouldn't be until the following year that he actually introduced his new drink, something called Pepsi-Cola.

Fiorello Henry LaGuardia was already thirteen years old by 1895; Robert Woodruff, five; and Wendell Lewis Willkie, three. But the world would have to wait another seven years for the births of Thomas Edmund Dewey and Arthur Flegenheimer—the former would eventually become famous, in the words of Alice Roosevelt, as "the little man on the wedding cake," the latter as a young mob boss named Dutch Schultz.

This, then, was the state of some of the events and some of the people who would influence my life. But of course I didn't know it at the time, and I'm not all that clear on the details, since I, myself, wasn't around until October 19, 1895. That fact alone leads me to think that, all things considered, it wasn't such a bad year.

We tend to look back on those times through a veil of mist as "the good old days," but I don't suppose they looked too good at the time if you happened to be born into one of the thousands of families who were living in New York in windowless, airless hovels. If, however, you were fortunate enough to be born into the solid middle class, as I was, it was a pretty good start—at least on the surface. And it was, I'd say, my first real stroke of luck.

No matter what one's circumstances, however, there was always a big question mark drawn over the "good" in those old days, since we certainly didn't have the facilities that we take for granted today. A doctor in Chicago had already performed open-heart surgery two years before, but what few hospitals there were in 1895 were there for the sick and the wounded, not for birthing babies. And so I was born into this world in the manner typical of the middle class at that time: I born in my father's house, a roomy brownstone on the Upper West Side of Manhattan. At the proper time the doctor came to the house, which had already been sanitized with clean sheets and plenty of hot water, and my grandmother was at my mother's side to help with the delivery. If there were any complications at the time, nobody ever told me, but we didn't talk about such things back then.

Although my parents met and married in New York, they came from different parts of the country and from very different backgrounds. My father's side originally came from Alton Junstadt, Bavaria, where they had been tailors for generations, so it was not surprising that when they settled down in Cincinnati they went into the woolen business. Over the years, they prospered enough to move to New York, where my father went to school and later into the textile business with his brother, my Uncle Harry.

But my grandfather on my mother's side is much closer to my heart. His name was Gustave Ranger, and he came over to this country from England two years before the Civil War. He settled down in what was then the little town of Galveston, Texas, and went into the cotton business with his brother. During the war they made a small fortune as blockade runners. They'd load up a chartered sailing ship with cotton and run it around the tip of Florida and up the Atlantic to the Northeast, where cotton was in heavy demand. They were merchants, to be sure, but more important, they were adventurers. At the end of the war Grandfather used his money to buy 3 million acres of virgin Texas land. It was priced at $2.50 an acre with only 50¢ an acre due on closing: not a bad deal, but it didn't work out. At the same time, he and his brother had cornered the entire cotton market in this country—the only two people ever to do so—but at the end of the war the British dumped all of their vast cotton holdings on the world market. As a result, Grandfather lost all his money, along with his big hunk of Texas. Still, the town of Ranger, Texas, was named after him, and I think I inherited some of his spirit of adventure and daring.

How my father and mother ever got together in New York I'll never know, but they did, and as a result I was born in that house at 312 West 71st Street. It was a typical brownstone in what was then a typical middle-class neighborhood of old New York, twenty feet wide by one hundred feet deep and exactly like every other house on the block. A twelve-stepped stoop in the front led into a gaslit vestibule that always seemed bathed in twilight. The ground floor, or basement, held the kitchen, laundry, and storage areas. The next floor, the first, had a dining room in the back and a parlor in front. The second floor was where my parents really lived, with a bedroom in the back and a library, where they spent most of their time, in front. The floor above, the third, was where I hung out. My bedroom was in the front, on the street; my sister's was in the back; and there was an extra bedroom, a guest room, for the ever present visiting relative. The top floor was where the servants lived.

There was a big bathroom on each of the upper three floors and one long staircase that went straight through the house, right up to the skylight ladder that led to the roof. One of my clearest recollections of that house and those early years is that it was one very long walk up to my room. The rooms were all very big and high, but they were hot and stuffy in the summertime and not exactly cozy in the winter. We were lit by gas, heated by coal, and cooled down in the warmer months by, at best, a glass of lemonade. It all seemed so simple and orderly at the time.

The house was staffed by a cook and a maid, and every Tuesday a laundress came in to do the washing, which was hung out on lines to dry in the backyard just like everyone else's on the block. The cook got a wage of around $30 a month, the maid considerably less, so naturally they didn't stay very long, and I recall a constant flow of fresh Irish faces cooking, cleaning, scrubbing, and running around our house.

I also remember the delivery carts that would start to appear at about six in the morning, with horses' hooves and iron wheels clattering over the paving stones under my front-room window. First came the milk delivery, then the rolls, and so on throughout the day. Everything was delivered to the front of the house and disappeared down into the basement. The iceman would rumble up with his big truck, calling down to each kitchen to find out how much was needed before hauling huge blocks out of his ice chest and carrying them on his shoulders down into the storage areas. In the warmer months these sounds and scenes would be clear and sharp in the bright morning air, but in the winter they were muffled by the snow, which to a youngster in old New York seemed to come fluttering down all winter long.

People didn't seem to have much money back then. At least *we* never did. We were reasonably well off by contemporary standards—not poor by any means, but certainly not rich—but then things were very cheap in those days, and we got along fairly well with very little. Taxes were nonexistent, and people could keep what they made and live frugally as well as comfortably.

Everybody on our block of brownstones knew each other, and the atmosphere was friendly and neighborly, with everybody ready to help one another out. If somebody was sick or died, everybody on the block pitched in. I remember the story of a man who came up from Georgia and bought a house on the block just to the north of us. One morning, soon after he had moved in, he woke up and looked out the window and saw a big black crape hanging over the door across the way. He went to his neighbor next door and asked who had died in the house across the way, but the neighbor said he didn't know. So he went to the house on the other side and they didn't know either. The next thing we heard, he sold his house and moved out because he wasn't going to live on a block where people didn't know who had died just across the street.

During the warmer months all the families took

chairs out in the evenings and sat on their front stoops and talked and visited with one another. In the winter, everyone would be out sweeping their steps or the street in front or shoveling snow, and we all seemed to work together. Each block of brownstones was more like a small village unto itself than part of a thriving, prosperous, driving city going through growing pains, and everyone had the time for neighborly pleasantries, something that's hard to find these days. The family was the center of everything back then, and as we supported our neighbors, we supported our relatives from out of town. Whenever they came to New York, they stayed with us. They didn't stay in a hotel, and as far as we were concerned there weren't any hotels in New York. We'd get word from cousins, aunts, nephews, or whomever, from Arizona or New Orleans, to say that they were coming into town for a few days on a shopping trip and did we have a bed available. And somehow we always did. It was usually the extra room on the floor where I lived, which remained closed except when somebody was coming for a visit. Then the maid would air it out, put sheets on the big double bed, and we'd know to expect a guest or two.

It worked the other way around, too, of course. If we were to visit their town we would stay with them; but we never did visit any other city, and as a result, my father didn't like the arrangement very much. He never stopped complaining that it cost a lot of money to put up and feed all those relatives, but my mother was very friendly and fond of the whole family, and as a consequence, a constant stream of out-of-town relations passed through my early years.

Although we never went relative visiting, we were

lucky enough to get away to the mountains for a month or so in the summer. When my father was a student at City College in New York he used to go up to the Adirondacks on summer camping trips, and early on he found one particular spot that he especially liked. It was on a high bluff overlooking Lake Placid and quite wild and deserted. He bought a lot up there for practically nothing and put up a log shack that was primitive but roomy enough for all of us, so when I was growing up we would all spend the month of August up there. It was reasonably cheap, which appealed to my father, and while it was what you might call very basic living, it was a blessing to leave the city heat behind.

To get there we would take a Delaware & Hudson train as far as Westport and then drive in a buckboard to the lake. From there a guide rowed us up the lake and we climbed up to the cabin. Compared to the ease with which we get around today, it was quite a trek for a city-dwelling family planning to stay for a month. Mother cooked our meals over a big wood stove, and if you wanted water, you slung a yoke, complete with a pair of buckets, over your shoulder and went down to the lake and fetched your own. It was nothing if not rustic, and I don't think it was exactly a vacation for my mother, but we youngsters loved it, and my father was content enough because it wasn't costing him any money.

My father was a very strict person, very demanding, a disciplinarian of the old German school. Everything had to be run on schedule, clean and tidy, at home and in his life. Mother had a budget to live by, and if she spent too much money he'd raise holy hell. He was the money earner, and he was in charge. He also made a habit of saving 50 percent of anything he made. If he had a bad year, then all of us had a bad year, because he was still going to save that 50 percent.

That is how he grew, and that's the only way he grew. He didn't build his business; he simply took his money and put it into the bank or bought safe securities. Along the way he had plenty of opportunities to make a lot of money, but he wouldn't take the slightest risk. If he had had any vision or courage he could have made a fortune, but instead he saved and saved and did without money so that he could have it. His attitude was that anybody who made a lot of money must be dishonest. They couldn't be rich if they hadn't indulged in some skulduggery or bits of bribing. He spent his entire life working hard, and he was a miser, and when he died he left my mother a very wealthy widow. But he had few friends to come to his funeral. He didn't do things, and he didn't make friends. My sister was about as close to him as anyone could be, but nobody could get very close because he was so straitlaced and spent most of his time either reading or collecting stamps, the only things he was interested in collecting besides money.

I received many a licking from him, but it didn't bother me all that much because I really didn't look up to him; I really didn't respect him. I walked out of that house at least three times before I was eighteen saying, "To hell with it; I'm not going to live under this regime," but each time my mother brought me back. I don't know how she put up with him, but now I know that we put up with him mainly for her sake.

My father's influence on me was enormous, but in a

negative sense. I certainly didn't want to be like him, and so I always took the opposite approach. Looking back, I know that my father never really got much out of life. He didn't try, he didn't dare, and he didn't really know anything about life.

I went to Public School 87, which was at the corner of 76th Street and Amsterdam Avenue, and was educated in an atmosphere where free education was something important—and good. There was no favoritism, and although the classes were big, all the kids did their homework and the teachers didn't put up with any shenanigans. Our principal was a man, the vice-principal a woman, and we held them both in awe. If you did anything wrong you would have reports sent home and your parents would have to bring you back to face one of these two figures of authority. If you caused trouble you would get a hell of a whaling—and I got a number of them—but if the atmosphere was strict, the education was excellent.

The streets were our playground after school and on weekends, since there wasn't much traffic to get in our way. Deliveries tapered off by the afternoon, and what trolleys there were ran up and down Broadway, which seemed a long way away. We all stuck pretty much to the block and all the kids knew one another. Stickball was our basic street game, but when we had a match game to play we would go across the tracks of the Hudson River Line, and play in the deserted lots on the far side. The HRL ran eight busy tracks between Riverside Drive and the Hudson River, and since it was the main freight delivery system into the docks and onto the lower West Side, they were busy tracks indeed, and crossing them could be dangerous, or at least it looked dangerous to our parents. But even though Riverside Park was just one block north, there was no place to play ball there, so we just went over the tracks and played on the far side anyway. It was against the law, and if we were caught we'd get a good tanning, but that never stopped us. Authority was something we respected and even feared, but that didn't mean we couldn't bypass it now and then.

Although we all played together, the boys usually stuck to the other boys, and the girls to the girls. We hardly ever came together, at least not in public. Our families were very strict about mixing it up too much, but anybody who thinks that teenage sex was discovered by the current generation had better think again. True, in those days we wouldn't usually go much further than heavy petting, but that seemed good enough at the time.

There was one very attractive girl from the family just two doors down our block—which is about as far as anybody strayed in those days—Maggie by name and just as cute as a button. For a girl of about fourteen, she had a particularly beautiful figure. I had a little fox terrier that I used to take out for walks every night at about seven or eight, and before long Maggie also got herself a little dog and we found ourselves walking them together in nearby Riverside Park. Soon after that the two dogs found themselves tied to a bench while we indulged in a little necking. It wasn't very serious, but it sure was a hell of a lot of fun, and it went on for about three months. Then one night her mother came out to the park looking for her and discovered the two dogs tied to the bench and the two of us in a passionate teenage embrace, and that was that. Maggie stopped taking her little dog for little walks.

One night not long after, she slipped me a note that said to meet her up on the roof after everybody was in bed. Of course all of those brownstones were connected, so it was a simple enough matter to climb up the stairs and through the skylight after everyone else was tucked in, and cross over the one roof that separated us. We never did go the limit, but we enjoyed many a night up on that roof. And her mother never guessed a thing.

The first person I really did sleep with, though, was not one of the girls on the block but my Aunt Nina from California. She was my mother's half-sister, and she was married. She was also thirty-five or more and I was just barely fifteen, but we made a good coupling of it while it lasted. She came east on one of her yearly shopping trips and stayed in the guest room right down the hall. On the first night of this visit I was headed for the bathroom and passed her open door. She had just taken a bath and was standing in front of the mirror powdering herself. I just stopped and stared, enthralled by her bosoms. Oh, it was a great sight.

Aunt Nina looked into the mirror and saw me standing there and smiled. "Why, Walter," she said. "You don't need to stand out there, just come in!" I remember her voice was warm, and at the time everybody else was calling me Junior and here she was calling me Walter. And those breasts! Well, needless to say, I went right in. Nina slipped on her nightie and got into bed. I sort of stuttered and stammered and said that I was just on my way to the bathroom, and she said,

"Why don't you go ahead, and stop in on your way back and we'll have a little chat."

That little trip to the bathroom was one of the longest journeys of my youth, but on the way back I went into the room, sat on the edge of the bed, and started our little chat—at least I think I did. The next thing I knew she had moved over in the bed, I was lying in there beside her, and we spent the night together. It was the first of our many nights together. She was supposed to stay for two or three days that trip, but she stayed for a week, and after that her once-a-year shopping trips to New York increased in frequency to about four times a year.

I never had the slightest bit of guilt about sleeping with Aunt Nina, but I wasn't too interested in having my family find out about it either. Not that I would have been ashamed at all, but that would probably have meant the end of her little shopping trips.

Up until that time I hadn't realized what I was missing, but Nina introduced me to a whole new world, opened up new excitements for me. And it was an exciting world that was to occupy an inordinate amount of my time in the years to come. From that day on, I never really looked at an attractive girl without wondering if I could sleep with her. Some I did, some I didn't, but it came as a great surprise in my early years that so many were so easy and that they all seemed to enjoy it as much as I did. However, most of the women I slept with were married, and most were older. I've slept with many different types over the years, but I don't think I've ever slept with a virgin. It's always been sort of against my ethics to start them off on something unless they had already decided for themselves and had tried it out on someone else. I suppose it's all because I had the good fortune to start off the right way. Thank you, Aunt Nina, wherever you are.

By the time I entered DeWitt Clinton High School I already felt that I was a man. I had experienced what few of the other boys had and was ready for anything —or so I thought. But while DeWitt Clinton provided the same environment for a good education as my elementary school had, it was a pretty rough school in a pretty rough neighborhood. It was on the corner of 59th Street and Tenth Avenue, smack in the middle of a lower-income district that we used to refer to as San Juan Hill because it was populated by Spanish-speaking families, and the kids from those families controlled the streets by roaming them in gangs. When we walked to school (and walk we did, because there were no buses, and even if there had been, none of us would have had the money to take them), we always went five to ten strong, and many is the time we had to fight our way through. We were the white boys from a middle-class district and we were invading their turf. It was rough and tough, but in a very short time I learned to be a street fighter, when to face it head on and when to avoid a conflict because the odds were too great. Those early lessons stayed with me over the years and served me well in business, where you can have everything in your favor on paper, but if you haven't got the street smarts and you haven't got the stomach, then you really haven't got it.

Once inside the school, though, it still wasn't a picnic. Bells rang every hour, and that meant you had to pass along the corridors and up the stairs to your next class, and that's when the real trouble started. There was a whole group of toughs who resented the people who had better clothes than they did, and during the time between bells they would snatch people's coats, hats, anything they could get their hands on, and if you squealed you got beaten up after school.

It all got really out of hand towards my senior year, and the principal of the school called a meeting of the various department heads to see if they could do anything about it. The athletic director was a big Irishman by the name of Doty, and he said that the only thing to do was to form a squad of students and let them police the halls during the changing of classes and after school. It was to be called the Doty Squad, and since I was vice-chairman of my senior class he made me a lieutenant in charge of forming the squad. I said that as far as I was concerned, I wanted to pick only the toughest boys, some of whom I knew were beating up the other fellows, and make them part of the Doty Squad. So I went out and gave these young gangsters the responsibility. I put them in the halls and literally made them change sides. We gave them a little gold badge that read "Doty Squad," gave each a beat—a staircase and a landing—and it went like clockwork. They policed the halls because they knew how to police them; they knew where the trouble was coming from. The whole thing cleared itself up in two weeks.

The Doty Squad was another early, lasting lesson for me. People who don't really have any responsibility, people who have nothing to do, resent the position they're in, so that often when you give them a position with some importance it changes their whole attitude. This may not always work, but over the years I've found that it's almost always worth a try.

2

I entered Harvard in the autumn of 1913, and suddenly
I was like a bird let out of a cage. Free at last, away
from my family and from the stifling atmosphere of my
father's house. Looking back, it's no small wonder that
I ever got to Harvard in the first place. At DeWitt
Clinton I was a pretty mediocre student right down the
line. I never really worked very hard at anything except
making friends. I seemed to get along well with
everybody, which made life more pleasant, but that
wasn't exactly designed to impress Harvard's admissions board.

And at the time it was very unusual for a New York
public school boy to get admitted to Harvard even if

he was an ace student with all the right credentials, which I certainly wasn't. They gave the entrance exam at the Harvard Club in New York, and quite a few boys from all over town took it—five from DeWitt Clinton alone—but only two of us in the entire city were accepted, myself and a fellow named Jimmy Seymour whose family was originally from Boston. Harvard was still very Back Bay then, and they didn't look upon you with great favor if you happened to come from New York. And I was Jewish, and there were very few Jews at Harvard in 1913.

Still, I passed the first hurdle, but there was a bigger one to come. My father. With his thriftiness, he naturally wanted me to go to NYU, but his brother, my Uncle Harry, came to the rescue. He was a lawyer who had gone to Harvard Law School, and since he didn't have any children and I was the only boy in the family, he offered to pay my way if my father refused. Well, they had a hell of a battle over that one, and the result was that my father's pride was assaulted and I went to Harvard at his expense. I think my whole first year there cost something like $400, which he certainly could afford, but he didn't like it one bit.

There were aspects of my early life in New York that I knew I would miss, particularly the friendship of all the boys on the block. It was their friendship that got me away from my family and allowed me a glimpse of how other people lived. And it was certainly very different from the way my family lived, since we didn't go to the theater or the opera or spend any money to enjoy the wonderful opportunities available to those living in New York in the early part of this century. My family just seemed to be living out its own peaceful, dreary life without getting any real pleasure out of it.

I was particularly unhappy with my father and with what I could see, even then, he was doing—or rather not doing. I watched other people on the block, men my father's age and in similar economic circumstances, and I saw them work and grow. They were buying and investing, taking a part in new and exciting things, and they prospered and grew with our young country. My father just sat back and saved and, as far as I could see, grew smaller. That part of my early life I was all too happy to leave behind.

When I first entered Harvard I didn't know a soul there. Most of the boys were from Massachusetts and they knew each other through their families, who had known each other for generations. It was like one big club, and I was a complete stranger; but in truth it didn't bother me in the least. I plowed right in, took as many courses as possible, and went out for everything in sight. I started out on the freshman crew, until they figured out what was wrong with the freshman crew; so I switched over to football, and although I didn't do very well, I was having a good time and meeting all sorts of people. As I went out for various things I soon found out that my talent was to a great extent in the managerial field so from early on in my freshman year I figured out that if I stayed behind the scenes I could get a lot more done and be of much greater use.

My first year was a bit complicated, since I roomed with a junior classman by the name of Laurence Kubie. He was a bookworm, and all he did was study. Later in life he became a famous psychiatrist and a disciple of Sigmund Freud, but he was a pain in the neck to live with, so I shed him at the end of my freshman year, and from then on Harvard was more fun.

I joined the Pieta Club, which was a pretty good one, and lived at Westmorly Hall, which was on what was referred to as the Gold Coast. Most of the boys I hung around with were from Boston families, and they'd take me home with them for holidays and weekends and I got to know the crowd pretty well. There was a war going on in Europe, and Germans were not all that popular even then, but if there was any prejudice against my German background—or my Jewish background for that matter—I never noticed it. Perhaps it was there, but if so I simply ignored it and it disappeared.

It seemed to me that the whole Back Bay bunch missed an awful lot in life because they grew up with such limited horizons and such narrow vision. Unless you were from an old Boston family and your mother knew somebody else's grandfather, you just didn't belong and never would. Basically, they hurt themselves because they were limited in their outlook and their approach. Later in life, when I was building companies and had openings, many of my friends from those days came around looking for jobs, but since they had lived such a secluded life, they had yet to see over the horizon. It was unfortunate, but I could only help a few of them because most didn't have anything to build on. They didn't have any real experience, and I simply couldn't find a place to put them. It was even worse later on during the Depression. A lot of them had gone into the financial field in Boston and on Wall Street, which was merely a continuation of their earlier life.

When that disappeared, there just wasn't anyplace for them to go.

Boston was supposed to be a very staid community, and the Boston girls, who wore flat heels and flat-fronted jackets, were supposed to be very conservative. And indeed, when I first met most of them they were very reserved. Once past that reserve, though, they went all to pieces. The wildest parties I've ever been to have been parties at the homes of these bluebloods and descendents of our Pilgrim Fathers, but they're that way only when among their own; outside, at somebody else's gathering they're just as cold as fish—you wouldn't think they had an emotion in the world. But go to one of their own parties and it's the damndest thing you ever saw.

Girls weren't allowed in our dormitory back then, but of course we still managed to smuggle them in without too much trouble. And life at Westmorly Hall was quite luxurious: one of the luxuries was that there always seemed to be plenty of good-looking girls around. There was a big swimming pool down in the basement of the Hall with a massive fireplace over on one side of the room. Tea and toast were served in front of the fire every afternoon, but the morning was when it was really fun. Every day before breakfast we'd go down for an early swim and we dried ourselves off before the fire; and many's the time we'd find a few girls who'd spent the previous night with some of our friends. We'd all go swimming together in the nude while somebody stood watch for any professor who might be on the prowl, and it really put us in a great mood to go to class.

Life was pretty good at Harvard then. The world may have been falling apart elsewhere, but I wasn't elsewhere, and as far as I was concerned it was all duck soup. I majored in economics, and found my studies such a cinch that I took enough courses and loaded up my program with enough credits to have graduated in three years. I must say that the education I got in the New York City public school system—where the classes were so large that the teachers had no time for you unless you knew your stuff—made Harvard seem easy, at least to get Bs and Cs, which was all I wanted. I had all the points I needed to come out with the class of 1916, and if my father had found out, that is exactly what he would have made me do. But of course he never *did* find out, and I did go back for my fourth year, mainly because I was having such a hell of a good time. I became manager of the Dramatic Society, head of the Speakers Club, and, in my senior year, manager of the football team. I may have been a lousy athlete, but I got my letter for management, and that's how I got to be a member of the Varsity Club.

My entire time at Harvard was filled with fascination and friendship. By going out for so many extracurricular activities as well as taking a great many classes, I got to know most of my classmates, and they were a good crowd. All of them seemed to come from wealthy families, but I was the oddball from New York City, a public school boy who somehow wasn't impressed by their background. We got along well, and at many of their parties, their girlfriends and sisters seemed to have more fun with me than with them and their reserved ways. When it came to our senior year I was one of three put on the Senior Committee to run the class. I suppose I was put on that committee primarily because I got along with everybody. People, even sons of bitches, didn't bother me, and they still don't. I found out very quickly in life that a lot of people are shy, and if you go 50 percent of the way with them, they'll usually go the other 50. But if you're timid, you'll never get to know anybody, because most people don't really loosen up until they know you pretty well. Somebody has to break the ice, and I was always a good icebreaker.

After graduation, most of my classmates went into banking or the brokerage business, continuing right on in the family tradition. Only a few of us—like Buckminster Fuller, who was from the Midwest but went to prep school in New England, and Roger Tyler, who was a New Englander but left the fold and went on to become a well-respected judge—really went out on our own. However, we were, and still are—what's left of us after sixty years—all good friends to this day.

During my four years at Harvard, I think the main thing I learned was how to study: how to organize my mind and how to find out about things. Everybody spends a lot of time at school acquiring an awful lot of academic information that just will not stay with you. The dates of various wars and battles or something like that. To hell with them. What difference do they make in the long run? I knew them once, and today I still know where to find them if I need to, and that's what's important. But how to go about intelligent living—that's what my schooling was all about.

I get a bit worried these days when the only things anybody seems to take are courses geared entirely towards a profession. That's fine, but what does that really teach you unless you first know how to live? I certainly wasn't the smartest boy in my class, and I didn't try to be, but I wanted to learn as much as I possibly could. And nothing stuck with me better than the lesson of how to organize myself and my learning so that it would contribute to the fullness of my life.

The other important thing I learned is that if you are going to grow and do things, you can't sit behind a desk and read a book. You have got to go out and expose yourself. Only then will you get results. I've never made a trip anywhere at any time that I haven't come back with a fresh, new idea. I used to travel a lot, and I always made a point of exposing myself to many different kinds of people, because by doing so, by exposing myself to them and to their thinking, I would gather information and ideas. You have got to see what's going on, you've got to feel what's going on, you've got to get the tempo, and you can't do that by sitting around at a desk or hemming and hawing while other people do it. I don't know if Harvard actually taught me that or if I just happened to learn it while I was there, but I'm willing to give credit where it's due —which just happens to be another thing I learned at college.

3

The war in Europe broke out in July 1914, between my freshman and sophomore years. At first it was regarded very much as a European conflict, and it took America a long time to get itself geared up to join the fight. Up until then our only real foreign involvement had been the short Spanish-American War, which had been regarded as a "jolly little fight," but the big one going on in Europe was pitting millions against millions in the bloodiest battles the world had ever seen. And not only did there seem to be very little progress on either side, but over here we weren't even all that sure what they were fighting about. Little wonder then that most Americans really wanted to stay out of the whole damn mess as long as possible.

Slowly, though, we did come around as a nation. When the *Lusitania* was torpedoed in May 1915 by a German U-boat off the coast of Ireland, it went down with 1,195 people including 128 Americans. It was probably one of the first major incidents to bring the "foreign war" home to our shores. Yet three days after she sank, President Wilson was still able to state, "There is such a thing as being too proud to fight," which reflected the majority opinion of the day. But at the same time, he sent a strongly worded warning to Berlin, and even that was too much for a lot of people, including his pacifist Secretary of State, William Jennings Bryan, who resigned in protest. Noninvolvement was still the ruling sentiment.

Within a year, however, that climate had changed considerably, and in October 1916, Wilson made a speech in which he said: "I believe that the business of neutrality is over. The nature of modern war leaves no state untouched." That pretty much summed up the growing mood of the nation, and although he won reelection in November, partially on the slogan, "He Kept Us Out of War," we knew we were heading into one very soon.

The actual declaration didn't come until April of my senior year, but by that time my class as a body was anxious and raring to go. Graduation was supposed to be held in June 1917, but it was decided to give special war degrees to all those who had been satisfactory up until that time and who wanted to leave early to join up. And of course everybody did; Harvard became a deserted campus. We never got around to a commencement that year, but since I was the only member of the class who already had enough points to graduate—as I could have done the year before—I was the only guy who got a regular degree and didn't have to return for a postwar commencement.

Since the war was being fought overseas, most of us thought that the action would be in the Navy, so a bunch of us got together and went up to Newport, Rhode Island, and enlisted. Because a lot of the Boston boys had spent most of their lives messing around in boats and knew a bit about sailing, they immediately became First Class Seamen, but as a city slicker from Manhattan, I entered boot camp as a Second Class Seaman, which is about as low as you can go in the Navy.

Newport wasn't really ready for us when we arrived, and at first we were billeted in tents. But a lot of the Harvard boys had friends and relatives who traditionally spent their summers in Newport, so that opened the town right up for us. Newport was a very strange place at the time. It was filled with enormously wealthy people who lived in vast mansions and led extravagant lives, yet for all of us future war heroes with good connections, the doors were opened wide. It was a continuous round of parties: cocktail parties, banquets, holiday balls, and especially coming-out parties for the debutantes who were tripping over themselves to be nice to the fresh infusion of new blood the war had forced upon their close-knit summer community. Well, we'd all arrive in our seaman's uniforms and just take over those parties, cutting in on the admirals and all the brass from the regular Navy, because the young girls would naturally rather dance with us than with a string of old men.

The main street of Newport was Bellevue Avenue,

and on it there was a club called the Reading Room that belonged to the wealthy men of Newport. It was in the middle of Bellevue Avenue, and right across the street there were branches of all the smart New York shops. In the summertime the models from New York, Boston, and all over would come out to these shops to work as salesgirls and enjoy the season, and part of their enjoyment was to be taken out by the rich men who were members of the Reading Room. All of these old codgers would tell their wives that they were going down to the Reading Room, and they'd go in through the front door and right out the back, and take out one of the models for the evening. We would see them all out on the town together, and the next night we'd go out with the models and spend the evening laughing over what these old goats had tried to do with them the night before. So, all in all, we did okay. The summer season in Newport was not too hard to take, even for a lowly Second Class Seaman.

After I graduated from boot camp I was promoted to First Class Seaman and recommended to go with a group of college graduates to Annapolis to take special training that would develop us into instant officers. The first class went down in midsummer, and I was to be a member of the second class, due there in September. It couldn't have worked out better for me, since it gave me the whole summer season in Newport.

One of my great friends at boot camp in Newport was a fellow named George Delacey. He had gone to Princeton instead of Harvard, but I didn't hold that against him in the least. He was a fine fellow. George had been in the first class to go down to Annapolis, and he knew that I was marked down for the second, so before I went he wrote me a long report of what to expect when I got there. He'd already been assigned to sea duty, but he included in his report a number of letters of introduction. The result was that when I arrived in Annapolis I was already right at home.

In a way, it was the darndest thing you ever saw. Here I was, a young sailor from up north, and the second day I was there I got a note from the wife of one of the captains who was out at sea. She said that George Delacey had told her to look me up and look after me and asked me to come over and see her at recess that afternoon. Recess was an hour off each day between roll calls at five and six o'clock, so I went over to see her at five o'clock that afternoon and she introduced me to a whole group of other officers' wives, and within no time at all I was one of the local crowd.

The commanding officer of the Naval Station was Admiral Edward Eberle, a nice old fellow with long whiskers. He lived with his granddaughter Ann, one of the most attractive and energetic gals I'd ever run across, in a big white house reserved for the commandant in the middle of the base. Again, I was introduced to her through a letter from George Delacey, so I've a lot to thank him for. I would take my hour's recess every day and run over to the admiral's house and sit there with his granddaughter sipping cocktails, just having the time of my life. The old admiral was a very strict disciplinarian, but then, what he didn't know didn't bother him, and it certainly made life a bit more pleasurable for a poor sailor.

When it came time for the big Army/Navy football game, I went along with the Eberles as Ann's escort, and it was one of the highlights of my little tour of duty in Annapolis. The admiral had a huge open touring Packard, and he sat up in front with his uniformed driver while Ann and I snuggled up under the bear rug in the backseat and held hands. I recommend this method of transportation to every seaman who wants to see the annual Army/Navy game in style.

Years later when I was on my honeymoon with my first wife, Marian, we were driving outside Zurich in one of those low, open horse-drawn victorias and who should be coming along in the opposite direction but Ann Eberle. She waved and blew kisses and paid no attention whatsoever to my bride sitting right there alongside me. She called out asking where I was staying, and I hollered the name of our hotel, and when we got back there was a note from her. Fortunately, I didn't open it in front of my wife. The note asked me to come over to her hotel that evening so that we could go canoeing by moonlight and have some fun for old time's sake. Well, I called her up and we talked, but I said that I really couldn't accept her invitation, since I was on my honeymoon, and that was that. I've often wondered what old flame we might have rekindled if we had gone canoeing that night, but I'll always remember that in those early days, she was the perfect girl to show me Annapolis.

America didn't go completely dry until January 1920, but the Navy was a few years ahead of the rest of the country on that particular score. The Secretary of the Navy, a Bible thumper from North Carolina named Josephus Daniels, had ordered the floating Navy dry in 1914, substituting Welch's grape juice for the traditional rum. Even in 1917, though, there was still plenty to drink at the shore bases, and possibly nowhere more so than in Annapolis. That was all to come to a thundering halt while I was there, however, when an order came down from the admiralty in Washington saying that all naval stations were to go dry immediately. From that day on there was to be no hard liquor allowed anywhere around Annapolis. It all had to be thrown out and the bottles broken. Or, it had to be consumed immediately, before midnight. That idea seemed by far the better, so Admiral Profit's wife decided to give one last party. Her husband just happened to be away at the time, and she neglected to inform old Admiral Eberle of the memorable event, but she was complying with the law. Her house was one of those sprawling monsters right on Annapolis Bay, and on the lawn behind, which ran right down to the harbor, she laid out a long line of tables. All the guests had to bring all the bottles they could find and put them on the table and then everything had to be consumed by midnight.

Well, it was the damndest party. I ever saw. Everyone was there—admirals, captains, I never saw so much gold and brass in my life—shoulder to shoulder with the ensigns and students from the academy. And, of course, there were plenty of girls and officers' wives. As soon as anyone arrived, they grabbed a sandwich and a drink and started downing as much as they could, as fast as they could, to get it out of the way before the midnight deadline. I started out early, and the next thing I knew it was getting light and I was sitting out on a bench by the sea wall but I wasn't seeing the sea very well. Then I remember Ann coming up to me and telling me that they had some rooms reserved at Carvel Hall, which was the only hotel in

33

town at the time. Somebody took me up to a room, took off my uniform, and I curled up and went to sleep. Okay, I passed out.

The sun, streaming into the room and into my eyes, woke me up the next day. I looked over and there was somebody in bed with me. His face was covered with whiskers and his body by long red underwear, and I couldn't figure out who or what it was, or what it was doing there. About that time he woke up, looked at me, and said, "Mack, what the hell are you doing here?" It was John Henry Newton, my senior professor in seamanship at the academy, and he and I were in bed together sleeping off the night before. Needless to say I passed my seamanship course first in the class.

My journey through Harvard, Newport, and Annapolis was my coming-out party to the world. I was in the best of places at the best of times, and it was through very little of my own doing. I know I couldn't have gone that far without an enormous amount of luck, but what I didn't know at the time was that the luck was going to stay with me for the rest of my life.

4

Somehow I managed to graduate from Annapolis third in a class of three hundred, and it wasn't entirely due to Professor Newton and his seamanship course. In spite of all the fun I had while I was there, I worked hard, harder than I'd ever worked at anything before; but then a lot of my courses were based on mathematics, and I've always had a knack for math. There's something very positive, very final about it that appeals to me.

Upon graduation we were all commissioned ensigns in the Naval Reserve, and I was briefly assigned to the USS *New Jersey* before being reassigned to the SS *Hamburg*, which was being refitted in New York Harbor. The *Hamburg,* an old luxury liner from the Hamburg-American Line, had the misfortune to be in New York when war broke out, so it was confiscated by the U.S. government to be used as a troop transport. She was completely refitted for war, stripped of all her luxury trimmings, and renamed the *Powhatan.* They certainly couldn't have a ship named the *Hamburg* transporting soldiers across the Atlantic to fight the Germans. Powhatan, the name of an Indian chief, seemed more appropriate.

We carried a naval contingent of about four hundred and fifty men, and we could transport up to ten thousand troops, though as a rule it was closer to half that number. It was a far cry from the luxurious transportation of the *Hamburg* days; the troops were stacked four to six high in sleeping hammocks, so if the guy on top was seasick, everybody knew it. And it was always the guy on top who got sick. That seems to be a law of the sea.

I was the senior junior officer and assistant navigating officer. In addition, I was put in charge of the after gun crew, which manned two six-inch guns and depth charges. I seemed to spend a lot of time in the aft crow's nest, which I wasn't really prepared for, but then there's no way anybody could prepare you for climbing up a flimsy Jacob's ladder while a ship is tossing this way and that in the middle of the Atlantic. But I was young and energetic and didn't realize how crazy and dangerous it really was.

I shared a room in officers quarters with a tough little guy named Butch McGee. He'd been a shortstop on the Yale baseball team, and I didn't think anything could faze him. But one day when he was up on watch in the crow's nest we ran into a hell of a storm and were rolling all over the place and McGee was just rooted to the spot up there. He was scared to death and just couldn't come down. In the end I had to send some of the toughest boys from my gun crew up to get him or he'd still be there.

We would load up with troops in New York or Newport News and head out in a convoy of about ten or twelve troop ships together with an escort of destroyers. The entire Atlantic was alive with German U-boats even then, and we had to follow a zigzag course the entire way. At night all the ships in convoy would scatter and go their separate ways and then try to rendezvous in the morning. And the nights were the worst. Of course, we had no running lights, no lights at all, and we had to maintain strict radio silence. So there you were, out in the black ocean all by yourself. It was very unnerving, I can tell you.

At first light, about four A.M., we'd all be miles from one another and easy pickings for any U-boat. That's when it was hardest to see a small periscope cutting through the dark water, and easiest to see a big troop ship, lumbering along at a top speed of twelve knots, silhouetted against the dawn. We didn't make a single trip without being shot at, but because of our zigzagging, we were never hit. And again, luck was on board with me.

We had a big lookout tower on top of the ship with a platform in which there were eighteen boys, each assigned a sector. They would just sit there with their binoculars pointed in one certain direction, able to move them only up and down, their eyes trained at the surface looking for a U-boat. It was tedious work, and they were relieved every half hour, but the funny part about it was that every time a telescope was sighted it would be by some sick sailor heaving over the side who just happened to pull his head up and see one coming at us. Invariably, that's how our submarine attacks were spotted.

Once we'd sighted one, we would signal our destroyers, drop a couple of depth charges, and get the hell out of there, zigzagging all the way. If one of our convoy was hit, we would all have to scatter immediately. It was not our job to pick up survivors. Once in convoy, one of the ships ahead of us, the *Mt. Vernon,* was hit, and following instructions we changed course and steamed right by her while she went down with over six thousand men aboard. The destroyers got in there fast and picked up a lot of survivors, but no doubt plenty were lost. Still, there was nothing the other troop transports could do. If one of us stopped to help, we'd just be sitting ducks waiting there for the U-boat to blow us out of the water.

It took about two weeks to make it across the Atlantic to our French port, either Brest or St. Lazar. There we'd spend two weeks unloading our troops, another two weeks reloading with wounded or returning troops, and another two traveling back to our U.S. port—six weeks in all. Once reloaded, a transport would head out alone—no convoy or destroyer escort for the return trip. We had nothing but our zigzag course to protect us.

On one trip we were about two days out of Newport News when we received a distress call: A tanker had been hit and its crew had taken to lifeboats. We were already headed for that location and would be there in two hours, so the captain called a conference and informed us that we were going to maintain course. His reasoning was that the location had already come up on the air, so everybody knew where it was. Since destroyers were already headed that way, the sub wasn't going to stick around. As a result, it would be the safest place for us.

So we headed directly for the spot where the tanker had radioed it had gone down, and as we came to it we could see a couple of lifeboats overflowing with men. It made me sick when we steamed right by them floating out there in the middle of the ocean at least a day from the nearest land, but we couldn't stop, not even for a few minutes. It was against regulations. The next morning we passed two destroyers headed out in their direction, and since the seas weren't too rough, I hope they found them. I'll never know for sure, but at the time it really bothered me.

Our captain on the *Powhatan* was a four-striper by the name of Murdock. He'd had a lot of battleship experience, and how they ever picked him for this troop ship I'll never know, but he couldn't have been a nicer guy. He and I shared the morning watch together, the sunrise watch, when we were at our greatest disadvantage with the U-boats. We'd walk that bridge back and forth together, our eyes glued to the surface of the water, and we got to know each other well. He would give me lectures and told me a lot about life, but one piece of advice he gave me stuck with me for the next sixty years.

"Walter," he said, "you're a young fellow with your

whole life ahead of you. I'm much, much older and I've been around, so I want to give you a fine piece of advice, and I don't want you ever to forget it. I've done a hell of a lot of things in my life; some of them were great and others didn't track so well, but I washed them out of my mind and they don't bother me. The only regrets I do have are over the things I could have done and never did, and now I'll never know what they would have been like and what I might have missed.

"Let me give you a good example. Years ago I was the military attaché stationed with the American embassy in Tokyo, and one weekend the Japanese secretary of state asked me to come out with the ambassador to his country place. I went out there and we all had dinner with the secretary's wife, who, by the way, was a beautiful little thing. After dinner the secretary and the ambassador went into another room for a private session and left me alone with the wife. She started showing me around the garden and then led me over to this little hideaway where she said we could have some fun. What she meant was that she wanted to have sex right there in the teahouse. I can tell you I was scared to death, because I thought it might cause a war or something. All I could think of was what would happen if it ever came out that while the Japanese secretary of state and the American ambassador were in private conference, the wife of one was copulating in the garden with the military attaché of the other.

"Well, I never did it, and to this day I've always regretted not doing it, because now I'll never know what it would have been like. Take my word for it, Walter. Don't go through life having any regrets about *not* doing something. Remember that little Japanese girl. Take everything as it comes along, because it will never come along again."

Captain Murdock was a real peach, and whenever we landed at Brest or St. Lazare or wherever, he'd go ashore and get reasonably loaded. I could always tell when he was drunk because he pulled the peak of his hat over his eyes so you couldn't see them and then he'd ask me what time it was. For some reason the only person he wanted to see when he was in this condition was me, so when he came back on board ship I always had to show up and walk him to his stateroom.

Brest was a very peculiar place when we first began to land there. The French resented our presence because our boys would go into town and take the girls away from the French sailors. Needless to say there were a lot more French sailors around than Americans, so they ganged up on our boys, stole their money, and beat them up. On our second trip we came in with a convoy of sixteen ships, and Admiral Williams, who was in charge of the Americans in Brest, called all the commanding officers ashore for a meeting. Captain Murdock returned from the meeting and announced that there would be no shore leave that night except for the officers.

I stayed on board, and when he came back about ten o'clock he had this little gleam in his eye, and I could see that he was loaded to the gills. He told me we were going to have a fire drill and instructed the bosun to sound the alarm. Well, at first I thought he just wanted to raise a little hell, but he really wanted a roll call, and sure enough he found out that a few of the boys had slipped off and gone ashore. They turned up about midnight all beaten up and a mess. They had been so outnumbered by the French that they didn't have a chance.

I guess the admiral didn't like the idea of his boys getting beaten up, because the following night we got a special order saying that everybody was to go ashore except for a skeleton crew, and that the uniform of the day was to be old dungarees. Everybody soon figured out why they were all being given shore leave at the same time, and the full crews of the sixteen convoys hit town dressed in their roughest clothes and cleaned that place up in no time at all. There were French sailors in hospitals for weeks afterwards. The next day the local chief of police came to our ship complaining that all his hospitals were overloaded and it was our fault, but from that day on we never had any trouble in Brest.

One time when we were anchored in Brest Harbor the captain boarded his gig, which was a small motor launch, and headed for shore to pick up the ship's orders. I was standing up on the bridge with the executive officer watching him go, and about halfway there that damn little boat caught fire. The exec looked around for an officer, and since I was the nearest one he yelled at me, "Mack, get out there with a crew in lifeboat #2 before that goddamn gig explodes." So I raced to the lifeboat and picked out the half-dozen biggest, strongest sailors I could for my emergency crew. I always figure that if you've got a hard job to do quickly you pick the strongest, most able-bodied men to do it, right? Wrong, at least in this case, because I had picked out the butcher, the baker, and a bunch of others who hadn't even the slightest idea how to hold an oar. When we hit the water it was a sight to behold. Here was this boat going around in circles in the harbor while six strong men flailed away at the water like they were playing with flyswatters.

By the time we finally reached the gig, the fire was already out and the captain was standing there with his arms crossed. He looked at me steadily for a minute before bellowing out, loud enough for the whole port to hear him: "Mack, just who the hell are you anyway? Don't you know anything about this man's Navy?" I spent another year on the *Powhatan* and I never did live that little incident down.

5

The war finally ended on November 11, 1918. It would be impossible to estimate the toll the previous four years had taken on civilization. Some 8 million were dead, while another 20 million had been wounded, maimed, or physically destroyed without the release of death, but the type of accounting that figures costs in the number of dead is as inhuman as the subject of that war itself. In Northern Europe there was revolution in Russia, in the south there were mass purges in Turkey, and all over the Continent alliances were shifting and retribution was harsh, mindless, and bloody. France, Germany, and Britain had lost an entire generation of their best and brightest young men, but we in

America got off relatively lightly. Only 120,000 of our boys lost their lives in that war. *Only* 120,000. War would never again be a "jolly little fight," as Teddy Roosevelt had termed it. The world into which I had been born had, for good or for bad, gone up forever in flames.

I was to stay on in the Navy until the latter part of 1919—there were still a lot of troops to ferry back across the Atlantic. When I finally did get out I found myself one of the millions who had lived for a time facing danger, even death, daily, never knowing what the next dawn would bring, and was suddenly thrown back into the lap of stability, mediocrity. For many of us the early twenties were, to say the least, a restless time.

I returned to New York and to my family, and for a time it seemed as if nothing had changed. My father was still the same old straitlaced disciplinarian, my mother was still easygoing, and the house was still stifling. There were great pressures on me to go into my father's business, a textile firm called Bedford Mills. It was a business that didn't interest me in the least, but my father claimed that he had built it for me, his only son, so I really had little choice.

During the war the entire textile business had grown tremendously. All the mills had speeded up production and put in a lot of new, additional equipment to take care of the government's massive orders for cloth. With the war over, however, there was a lot of extra mill capacity and an enormous surplus of machinery throughout the industry. My father's company, which had its major investment in a mill in Fall River, Massachusetts, was no exception, and it was a company

45

in trouble. This, at least, did interest me, but only if I could work it with a free hand. I couldn't, of course; but it took me a few years to find out that my natural gift for getting a company out of trouble and putting it back on its feet again was not wanted in my father's company. He was so busy saving, he couldn't even save his own company.

Since I didn't know anything about the textile business, I started out at the bottom with Bedford Mills as a door-to-door salesman. We dealt mostly in men's shirt material and cotton for women's underthings, so I carried sample bags from store to store, manufacturer to manufacturer. I quickly became assistant sales manager and finally general sales manager of all of Bedford Mills, but it was in spite of the fact that I was my father's son. The old man didn't think I would move ahead as fast as I did, but I found sales fascinating. I loved to go around meeting different people and trying out different approaches with them, and as a result I became a first-rate salesman.

All my life, in all the businesses I've been in, I first studied the sales side of that business, because no matter what business it is, if it doesn't have sales, it isn't a business. You can always get plenty of experts to run the mechanics and take care of production, but if you can't sell the product then you go under. And this holds true no matter what your product may be. Sales is the guts of any business, so before I ever went into anything I always looked first at what it was they were trying to sell, why they were trying to sell it, and if it had a place in the market.

After I'd been with Bedford Mills for three or four years I could see that the textile industry was changing. The New England mills were closing down all over the place and everyone was moving south, where they would be closer to the raw source, the cotton, and labor was cheaper. New England had once been a great center of manufacturing because of its early abundance of cheap labor; and with all the waterfalls and rivers around, there was power aplenty. But in the twenties the pendulum began its swing to the South, and anybody who couldn't see that was blind.

Moreover, my father's mills were turning out about twenty different kinds of shirting materials—percales, broadcloths, oxfords, and such—but to make short runs and change the looms frequently was expensive. If we specialized in just one or two weaves and ran the looms constantly, we would be able to produce a better fabric at a competitive price. It was simply a new approach to fabric manufacturing, and to my mind the only approach.

So I went to my dad one day and said to him: "You have got to do two things with this business if you're going to grow. First off you have to go south, buy up a cotton mill, and transfer all your manufacturing down there. Close up Bedford Mills; it's dying. They've got much cheaper labor down there because there are no unions, and they're close to the source of cotton so there are no transportation costs. Unless you move, the cheaper cotton manufacturers are going to put you out of business. And number two, there's tremendous overcapacity in this field, and unless you begin to specialize, you're going to be sunk."

Well, the old man just looked at me and said, "You know, I've been in this business for over thirty years and you've been around it for three, so you've got a hell of a lot of nerve coming in here telling me how to run it." And that was that. As it turned out, of course, I was right, but it took him another three years to realize it.

Working for my father was bad enough, but living in the same house with him was driving me crazy. It was also driving me out of the house, but I was lucky enough to channel my frustrations into a positive direction: charity and community work, and politics.

Greenwich House, a handsome building that was—and still is—at 27 Barrow Street in Greenwich Village, was part of a community project run by a wonderful woman named Mary Simkhovitch. She was a big, strong, tireless woman who did a great job looking after the sailors on shore leave in the Village during the war, which is when I first met her. She had saved a bunch of my boys from the Shore Patrol, and we struck up a friendship that was to last for years. She sensed that I was at loose ends around this time and talked me into coming down to help out with the kids who were running around the streets, getting into trouble. I'd go down to Greenwich House about three evenings a week and hold informal classes in which I'd try to teach the kids some of the things I'd learned at Harvard and in the Navy. It was pretty much a question-and-answer situation, and afterwards we would often go play ball in the street. I was almost like a camp counselor, only on the kids' own home territory. I think I did help in many little ways, and I know I certainly felt good about it.

I've never regarded myself as a particularly noble person—fair might be a better description—but I have always been very involved with the community. I feel we can't just take out, we have to put something back in, we have to keep feeding ourselves. That's what the community is all about, and that's why from very early on I have devoted a lot of time and energy to community organizations, and I believe it has all been time and energy well spent. To be perfectly honest, I really enjoyed working on community projects with people I'd otherwise never have met. The wealthy snobs miss a lot in life by never letting their hair down. I wanted to let mine down while I still had some to *let* down.

At about the same time, I started getting involved in politics—and originally for the same reason: to get out and away from my family. But once I was involved, politics became a new passion. By 1920 my parents had moved over to the East Side and we lived in the 17th Assembly District, where quite by accident I became a Republican. I was a liberal then and I'm a liberal now, and in the beginning I could have joined either the right wing of the Democratic Party or the liberal Republicans, but I chose the latter. New York was a solid Democratic bastion at the time, but the Republican Party seemed the solid party of the future.

I got involved with a captain of the 17th District and started spending a good part of my time at Republican headquarters on the East Side. The 17th was known as the Silk Stocking District, because it was controlled by a very wealthy area, right in the middle, and those people wore silk stockings; it's as simple as that. I soon became a lieutenant in the district, and in 1924 they elected me president of the Silk Stocking Club. We raised a lot of money, which I was pretty good at, bought ourselves a clubhouse on 83rd Street, and became the most powerful Republican group in the city. Of course, Jimmy Walker was the mayor down in City Hall, and Al Smith the governor up in Albany, and the real power in New York politics in those days was held by Tammany Hall and by the bootleg mobsters who had divided up the city. Nevertheless, we had a lot of money in the Silk Stocking District and wielded a lot of influence even then.

By 1924 my course was pretty well set, and it was channeled to take me down the two routes that would dominate my life for the next fifty years—business and politics. It was still my father's business, but I was learning; and it was still small-time local politics, but we were building; and my future was charted. I still had one problem, though. I was still living in my father's house, and marriage looked like the best way out of that one.

6

Marian Reckford was an extremely attractive girl and a lot of fun to be with, but I really wasn't thinking of marriage when we started running around together. In fact, it was one of the last things on my mind, since I wasn't in love with anybody. I was sort of seduced into it, though, by the glamour that surrounded her family. She was the granddaughter of Adolf Lewisohn, and he was one of the greatest guys I've ever met in my life.

Lewisohn had made a fortune out of the Amalgamated Copper Company, and he certainly knew how to spend it. He was a great philanthropist—Lewisohn Stadium was one of his gifts to the city of New York—and he was a high liver. He had an enormous estate in

Ardsley, New York, and he used to ask me to come up for weekends with Marian. He had three daughters, and they all had daughters—Marian was his eldest daughter's eldest daughter—and everybody gathered up there for weekends with their husbands, boyfriends, whatever, and we all had a ball.

Lewisohn was in his mid-seventies at that time, but you'd never have known it. He was full of energy, especially when it came to playing around. Even then he was keeping two separate mistresses. His chauffeur, who had been with him for years, became a great friend of mine and used to tell me stories of how the old man would take his ladies out in his big touring car, and while the driver stayed up front, Lewisohn would be in the back with the blinds pulled down playing around with his latest. Whenever they saw that chauffeur-driven limousine touring around the country roads near Ardsley with the blinds down in back, everybody knew what was going on.

Marian and I had been hanging around together for quite a while. I was twenty-nine, and in the crowd that we ran with, everybody got married sooner or later. Her family indicated to her that rumors of our engagement were flying, and one day she just called me up and asked if they were true, and I thought, "Why not?" Here was this attractive girl with millions and a great grandfather, and there didn't seem to be anybody else around I was more interested in, so I told her to go ahead and announce that we were going to get married. The fact that she asked me didn't really make all that much difference, since it wasn't a great romance in the first place.

When I told my father, he was very much against

the marriage. I don't know if he thought I was going to leave his business or what, but he said that she was a very nervous, excitable girl and that insanity ran in her family. He claimed that those things were hereditary, so that we would never be able to have any children. I thought, To hell with it. But for once my father was right. It was a terrible marriage, we never did have children, and she started to go to pieces soon after—but the wedding itself was terrific. Lewisohn threw a beautiful party out in the garden up in Ardsley, gave her wonderful presents, and lavished every affection possible on the two of us.

That was in 1924, and over the next few years Marian and I tried to have children, but it never worked. We had four, and all four died: two were stillborn and two lived only a short time after. Her doctor confided in me that the same thing had happened to her sister and advised that neither of the Reckford girls should attempt to have any children. Apparently the family was on its way out.

Marian was never interested in sex anyway. To her it was a bore. She was an intellectual. She enjoyed books, music, art, and money—boy, did she love money —but that was it. She told me quite frankly that she didn't care what I did as long as I came home to her for supper and was available to escort her to the proper places at the proper time. Appearances were all that mattered. Marriage to her was a bit like being stuck with a roommate you really didn't like all that much. As a result, I have to admit that I started playing around a lot.

Throughout this whole period I was in the habit of going down to the Harvard Club in the evenings to play squash, and all the boys down there were having a wonderful time buying and selling securities and making hundreds of thousands of dollars. One would say to me that he has bought some securities and sold them the next day and made $35,000 on the deal. Another one of my pals told me that if I bought stocks through him he would guarantee me ten points in two months. I didn't know anything about the market or anything about Wall Street, but this was boom time. Everything was going up and up, and there wasn't a thing you touched one day that wouldn't be worth more the next. And here I was working my tail off just to keep my head above water in a textile business that was sinking fast.

My father finally retired from Bedford Mills in 1927 and turned the business over to me, and although he really didn't turn over much besides a lot of work and no chance of ever making any money, it was just what I was waiting for. I liquidated what assets there were within five months, turned over the $200,000 that I got from the liquidation to my father—which was the amount of money he had left in the business from his original investment—and with my debts to him cleared up, I went out on my own.

Almost immediately I got a job with Otis & Co., a Cleveland-based brokerage firm whose New York office was headed by a fellow by the name of Floyd Eberstadt. I obviously got the job because I had connections and friends in the investment business, and they tried to put me in the Customer Service Department selling securities. That's the last thing I wanted. I went down there to try to go into the New Business Department, where they took companies and merged them. I wanted to build, to do constructive work; they wanted me to push securities to my friends, particularly my wife's friends and family; and they were willing to pay me $30,000 a year to do it. Still, I looked on it as a short training period and thought things would improve.

At the end of the first month, Mr. Eberstadt called me into his office, congratulated me on how rapidly I had caught on, and handed me my first paycheck for $2,500. I looked at the check—which was a hell of a lot of money then—and said: "Mr. Eberstadt, I didn't earn this money, and I'm not doing the work I want. I want to be transferred to the New Business Department. I'm interested in refinancing and reorganizing, not in being a customer's man." His answer was not to worry about it; I had earned the money and would go a long way as a customer's man, since that's where my future lay. My answer to him was to take the check, rip it up into little pieces, lay it in his ashtray, and walk out the door. My first paycheck and I just tore it up. Well, I guess I was a stubborn son of a bitch even then.

Luckily I'd saved a little money from when I was working for my father, so I could manage to get by. I suppose at the time everybody assumed I was able to make such a gesture because I had a rich wife, but I'd made it very clear to Marian before we married that we were going to have to live on whatever I earned and not touch one cent of her money. And I always lived up to that.

One of my classmates at college, William B. Nichols, had a small brokerage business downtown, and they'd been after me for some time to come join them. They dealt almost exclusively with original financing for small companies, and that appealed to me, so that's where I ended up.

Those were the days when investment trusts were just beginning to be formed—people would buy the stock of the investment trust, the officers of that trust would be responsible for investing the funds in market securities, and as the value of the securities grew, the value of the trust itself would grow—and Bill Nichols had just started one, a small fund called Chain & General Equities. It specialized in discount and chain stores, such as Woolworths, and supermarkets, such as Safeway and Grand Union, which were also just coming into their own. Soon after I started with Chain & General I met Charlie Merrill, a broker with Merrill, Lynch, and found him interested in financing these new, growing chains of stores through the sale of our investment stock. Together we prospered enormously. Of course, everything was prospering enormously back then, but in the great financial shock which was just around the corner, Chain & General, and those houses such as Merrill, Lynch that had handled our stock, would prove much more depression-proof than most.

II

The Boom and Bust of the Twenties and Thirties

7

The twenties was a great time to be around if you were lucky enough to be young and healthy and able to pay your own way. And it was especially fine if you happened to live in New York City. Again, I was one of the lucky ones.

Prohibition was the game of the day, and Texas Guinan was hosting speakeasies, selling bootleg booze for $25 a fifth and greeting us all with a democratic "Hello, sucker." Saks opened its classy doors on Fifth Avenue and on the very first day of business sold out its entire stock of silver pocket flasks, while farther up the street, Bergdorf Goodman moved into a new marble palace on the site of the Cornelius Vanderbilt II mansion.

On Broadway we laughed to George S. Kaufman, Noel Coward, Philip Barry, and S. N. Behrman, while Maxwell Anderson and Sidney Howard made us think and Eugene O'Neill made us wonder. Rodgers and Hart were writing our show tunes, while Ziegfeld's Follies and George White's Scandals kept us amused and dazzled. We sang "Tea for Two" and "Yes, We Have No Bananas" and, most of all, "I Want to Be Happy," and we played as hard as we thought we worked.

Prohibition had grown into an estimated $4 billion-a-year industry by 1926—the year that Al Capone's income was said to be $105 million, far higher than anybody else's—and when Calvin Coolidge said, "The business of America is business," we all agreed and turned up the jazz a little louder.

Soon after Marian and I were married, we bought a house at 14 East 94th Street, but after Marian's two stillbirths there we wanted to put the memory of the place behind us so we moved out and rented the house. Our first tenant turned out to be George S. Kaufman.

I didn't know the Kaufmans or any of their crowd before that chance business arrangement, but we all soon became fast friends, and they opened up a whole new world to me. But since I hardly ever went home anymore except to sleep now and then, it was a world I was never able to share with Marian.

George and Beatrice Kaufman gave brilliant dinner parties at that house on 94th Street; all the wits of the day seemed to be in residence, and after supper we'd sit on the floor and roll dice until dawn. The talk was fast and furious, and a lot of it went right over my head, but we were all having a whale of a time.

I remember that one night some friends of Beatrice's

were sailing for Europe, and we all trooped down to the ship and gave them a great big going-away party. I never thought so few people could drink so much champagne in such a short time, but somehow we managed, and we got off the boat just in time. At least most of us got off. Dorothy Parker got quite tight and passed out in another cabin, and the ship sailed off with her on board. Nobody knew anything about it until they found her the next morning, but by then they were too far out to sea to do anything about it.

So Dorothy landed in England with no suitcase, no passport, no money, and nothing to wear but the clothes on her back. When she returned from London the Kaufmans gave her a welcome-home party, and I well remember somebody asking her what she did in London for four days without any money or a change of clothes. She came back quick as a whip, "Oh, I spent most of my time sliding up and down barristers." She may have been polishing that line during her entire return voyage, but the delivery was perfect. They were all like that. Their minds were sharp, and they played off each other, so whenever anything came out, it sounded spontaneous when often it had been honed to perfection well beforehand. True charm, it seems, is always premeditated.

This was the heyday of the speakeasy, and we'd all gather in the smart ones on 52nd Street. One night I took Dorothy to one of the crowd's favorite watering holes, a place called Tony's, and Robert Benchley, Heywood Broun, and Alexander Woollcott were there with Beatrice Kaufman. Quite a heady crowd for a simple businessman like myself, but with enough drinks on the table it didn't seem to matter. Needless to say we all got quite loaded, and while the four heavy wits bounced their lines off each other, Beatrice and I said our good-nights.

In the taxi on the way home I knew that we were both as tight as ticks in summertime, and I was about to drop her off at the house on 94th Street when she said, "Walter, come on in for a minute and we'll have a little nightcap."

So we went in, and I remember distinctly putting my straw hat down on the table in the entrance hall as we walked up the first flight of stairs to the parlor. At that time the Kaufmans were as usual living *à trois*: George sleeping with his favorite beautiful girl of the moment on the second floor while Beatrice was on the third. But then these were very sophisticated people in a very sophisticated age, so it didn't bother me in the least.

"You fix yourself another drink, Walter. I'm just going upstairs a minute to get into something comfortable." And with that, Beatrice started to make her wobbly way upstairs. Now, Beatrice was a wonderful woman, but she was quite stout, and I never thought of her as anything other than a good pal. She evidently had something else in mind. I fixed myself that drink and was just at the point of drinking it when I looked up to see Beatrice Kaufman coming down the steps in a long black nightgown that was all open in the front and so sheer that you could see everything right through it. All I could see was this terrifically husky woman without a stitch on floating towards me. Luckily she was so drunk she had to hesitate a little at each step so she wouldn't stumble, and I took that as my cue to get out fast, grabbing my hat on the run as I left.

I didn't run into her until about a week later. She asked me what had happened, and I said, "Well, you know, Beatrice, I felt that I'd had more than enough to drink, and when you went upstairs I didn't know if you were ever going to come back down again, so I thought I'd better go." She never knew I'd seen her heading towards me that night, so we remained friends, although I guess old Captain Murdock would have said that's one of the things I missed and will never know about. But then again, I don't regret it in the least.

Soon after I became president of the Silk Stocking Club I got a call from the White House. The President's secretary said that Mr. Coolidge would like to talk to me about some Republican policies and could I come down and see him, so I put on my hat and headed for Washington. Coolidge was a good Republican and I respected him, but most of all I was flattered that he'd want to talk policy with me. True, our club was rich and influential, but it represented only a small district in the middle of a big Democratic city and state.

My appointment was for five, so I went in and waited for him at the end of his busy day. He had a lot of people to see before me and I didn't get in until about six, but he greeted me like an old friend, had me sit down, and we started talking politics. He said he wanted to get the Silk Stocking Club to endorse Ogden Mills, a distinguished member of our club for Secretary of the Treasury, since it would be better politics, and thus make it easier for Mills to get that appointment, if he first had the endorsement of the district he came from. I said I didn't have the slightest problem with that and we would be glad to endorse Mills. Then we talked a little more about politics in general and he thanked me for coming. As I got up to leave, his secretary, a handsome, white-haired fellow named Larry Ritchie, came in and whispered something in his ear. Coolidge just looked up at him and said, "Tell that boy scout to wait."

That's all I heard. Ritchie left, and I left a few minutes later, and the only person in the waiting room was the guy he had called a boy scout, Herbert Hoover, who at the time was in Coolidge's cabinet as Secretary of Commerce.

I was very fond of Coolidge. He was to the point, he didn't waste words, and the country prospered while he was around. He really did believe that the businessman was the backbone of the country, but I think he probably did a little too much for business. Perhaps if he had put the brakes on a bit sooner, we wouldn't have had such terrific speculation and such a wild run on securities. He got us moving a little too fast and furious, and then when he stepped aside with his famous "I do not choose to run" remark, his boy scout took over, and he couldn't handle the reins at all.

The funny part about it was that Hoover was probably one of the best-equipped men in the country to be President. He had a fine education, he was an excellent engineer, and his war relief work was superb, as indeed was his entire record of public service. But it was all on paper. He turned out to be one of the worst Presidents this country has ever seen simply because he could not handle people. He didn't understand people and he didn't care about them. He cared only about what he thought was the correct way of doing things. Coolidge saw that in him, and that's why he called him a boy scout.

Hoover isn't the only politician who looked good on paper and turned out to be a disaster in office. Another example was a guy named Nathanial Miller, a Harvard graduate and a brilliant lawyer, one of the finest lawyers in Wall Street. The Republican Party ran him for governor of New York, and he made one of the worst governors we've ever had. He simply didn't know how to handle people, was always at loggerheads with the Assembly in Albany, and he couldn't get anything done. Right after him came a guy from the sidewalks of New York with no education to speak of, and he made one of the greatest governors this or any state has ever had. His name was Al Smith, and his only secret was that he knew people and loved them.

It isn't so much being a politician that makes a man function in office; it's more a matter of handling situations that are continually changing without irritating other people. Not only did Hoover fall to pieces when the situation got out of hand, but he was irritating on a daily basis. I worked for him in 1928 and helped to get him elected, and soon after he was in office he sent for me and I went into that same office where a few years before I had gone to meet with Coolidge.

Hoover didn't look at me once, not even when we shook hands, which for me was a bit like shaking hands with a wet, cold fish. He wanted the Silk Stocking Club to endorse a judge he had picked, but all the while we talked he was drawing little designs and figures on a yellow pad and he never once looked me in the eye. It made me so mad that I had to use all the control I had not to walk out of the room. I was so irritated that I felt like opposing him no matter what he wanted. I'm not going to blame the entire Depression on Hoover, but almost anybody in America could have handled the Presidency better than he did, and in doing so might have made less of a disaster out of a disastrous situation.

A very good friend of mine, Ed Anthony, left his job as editor of the *Woman's Home Companion* to go down to Washington to act as Hoover's public relations secretary, a thankless and impossible position if there ever was one. When the famous Bonus Marchers, a group of 25,000 unemployed ex-soldiers, marched to Washington in the spring of 1932, Anthony went in to see Hoover and said, "Mr. President, the marchers will be in our park shortly, and I suggest that you order the Army to put up tents for them and feed them, and then ask them to form a committee to come and talk to you."

Without even looking up, Hoover said: "Mr. Anthony, these men are violating the law. They have no right to march on Washington, and I'll order the Army to drive them out of here."

Anthony tried again. "Mr. President, I think that would be a great mistake. These people are veterans, they're unemployed, and they're starving. They're suffering, and you ought to meet with them to see if there is anything we can do."

"Mr. Anthony, they are in open rebellion, and I am going to drive them out of Washington."

"Mr. Hoover, if you do that, then I had better resign."

Hoover finally turned and looked at him and said, "Mr. Anthony, I have just accepted your resignation."

Ed Anthony returned to New York, and on July 28, General Douglas MacArthur led a combined cavalry and infantry charge backed up by tanks, gas grenades, and machine guns to disperse the hungry crowd. Until the end, Hoover maintained that the Bonus Marchers were communists and persons with criminal records.

8

The Republican Party was not much of a party at all in New York City during the twenties. Statewide, it had some strength, but the city was completely controlled by Tammany Hall, and what passed for the Republican Party was really just the back door into Tammany Hall. The only exception to that was our district, the 17th, but we were a minority even in our own party.

The biggest problem with the party was its chairman, Sam Koenig, who was a Tammany Hall lackey on the side. He made deals all along the line, from judges to candidates, and never really contested any city election. It was a complete sellout. So when I got to be president of the Silk Stocking Club and saw what was really going on, I put on my reformer's hat and set out to do something about it. I went downtown to Koenig's office and told him that as far as I could see we were simply selling out, running a bunch of dummies for office who didn't have a hope in hell of getting elected to anything. I insisted that it was about time we built an organization and attempted to make the two-party system work. He just laughed at me.

"Sam," I said to him, "I'll give you two choices. Either you resign right now, or you agree that when you come up for reelection in 1928 you'll step aside gracefully and let us appoint someone who can clean up this party and reorganize."

That gave Sam his biggest laugh yet. "Walter, everybody's tried that one before and it's never worked, so forget it. Go back home and earn yourself some money."

With that we parted company, but I was fired with the determination to get him out of office by 1928. Wherever I went, they said it couldn't be done, but I mobilized my forces and gathered a war chest. Ogden Mills, whom I'd helped get appointed, was a large contributor, as was Ruth Pratt, the wife of one of the founders of Standard Oil and the first congresswoman to be elected from New York State, so by the time the vote came around in '28, there was practically nobody left to back Koenig. Nobody had bothered to oppose him before; he was just a straw man in the party, and he fell with ease.

I didn't want to go in as the new chairman—I was finding that, just as in school, I was much better behind the scenes—so we put in a young Harvard graduate named Chase Mellon. He served as county chairman, and I was his treasurer, and together we really reorganized the party and revitalized the Young Republican Organization, which up to that time had been pretty inept. We made a viable party out of what we had to work with and became instrumental in influencing the state's party politics. It was the first time anybody could remember that the New York City branch of the party was taken seriously.

The state chairman in those days was Frank Tanner, a hell of a nice fellow, and we used to get together and try to put up a balanced ticket when election time came around. We tried to get different types of people from different areas so that we'd have all elements covered. I remember once we were putting together a state ticket when Tom Dewey was running for governor, and we had pretty well covered all geographical areas, religions, and minorities when we suddenly realized that we didn't have a Jew on the ticket and we didn't have anybody from Buffalo. So here we all were sitting around at three in the morning tired as hell, and Kingsley Macy, who was by then state chairman, called up the Republican leader in Buffalo and said, "Sam, who have you got up there who's Jewish that we could run for state attorney general." And the guy from Buffalo said he didn't know offhand since it was the middle of the night but he'd think about it. "Well, think about it quick," said Macy, "because we need a Jew from Buffalo and we need him now."

A few minutes later he called back and said there was a lawyer he'd heard about who was head of the Jewish Relief in the area and he thought his name was Bernstein but that's all he knew. So we got this lawyer named Bernstein on the telephone at about four-thirty

in the morning and told him that we were going to
nominate him for attorney general on the state ticket,
and Bernstein came back with, "For Christ's sake, I
don't want to be attorney general. I just want to go
back to sleep." We finally talked him into running, and
he did become attorney general. That's the way the
tickets were put together back then. It really did happen in smoke-filled rooms, and it always seemed to be
four in the morning.

In 1932 I was asked to run for state senator from the
17th District, which extended from Washington Square
up the East Side to 116th Street. New York City was
then, as it is now, very much composed of a series of
small villages, or inner cities, and my district was a
perfect example. On the Lower East Side it was mainly
Italian and Jewish, and then around 26th Street it
turned into a Greek community. Midtown was primarily middle class and upper income—this is the area
that gave the district its handle, Silk Stocking—while
the Upper East Side was an entirely different inner
city composed primarily of a mixed foreign population.
Running for office was a great experience for me because I had to get around and make speeches and meet
the people in a totally new way. I spent a lot of time
above 96th Street getting to know the Italians and the
Spanish-speaking residents—primarily Puerto Ricans—
who lived in the area. It was during the summer, and
it was a hot one, and I think I spent half my time
climbing up fire escapes and sitting on front stoops. I
kissed an awful lot of babies that summer, although I
tried not to kiss too many under the age of sixteen.

Prohibition was still around, of course, and New
York City, like most every other city in the country,

was divided up into districts run by liquor lords, the bootleggers. Each had a district he controlled, and they ran their kingdoms as they saw fit. All the local politicians and the police were in on the take, and things ran smoothly until one of the district bootleggers got a little too ambitious and invaded the next guy's territory. That's when gang warfare broke out. But on the whole, New York was pretty well run in *that* respect at least. I'd never met Dutch Schultz, but everybody knew he was the liquor lord for the whole upper section of Manhattan, which included the top twenty blocks, from 96th to 116th Streets, of the district for which I was running, so I felt pretty sure that we would eventually get together on some basis.

The call came towards the end of that summer. I was still working for William B. Nichols, running Chain & General Equities, and one morning my secretary came into my office and said there were two strange-looking men outside who wanted to see me. I've always made it a policy to see anybody who came by, so I told her to send them in, and in walked these two tough-looking, heavyset characters. They said that Mr. Dutch Schultz would like to meet me, and I said I would be glad to meet him, so they said they'd pick me up the next morning at my apartment at nine A.M.

The next morning I emerged from my building at Park Avenue and 92nd Street to find a huge armored car waiting for me. The driver was a frail guy, standing about five-four, who introduced himself as Tom Brown. I sat up front with him and noticed while we were driving along that he was missing the third finger of his right hand. I later learned that he was Schultz's best trigger man because he didn't have this finger to get in his way and he could shoot fast. A few months later he was credited by the police department with being the man who shot the gangster Vincent Cole, and Brown himself was subsequently shot to death in a telephone booth on the Upper East Side. But all of that came later, and on this bright, hot summer's morning he was just a nice little guy who happened to be missing a finger.

Brown drove me up to a billiard hall at 116th Street and Seventh Avenue, where, after going through several doors, I found myself in a back room with a lot of tables. We sat down, and a few minutes later seven or eight men came in and we all shook hands. It was even hotter in that back room, and as we all took off our jackets, I noticed that I was the only one who wasn't wearing a leather shoulder holster and revolver. A few minutes after that, Dutch Schultz joined us. He was only thirty at the time, but he was a big, flabby fellow, and extremely jovial, at least with me. He asked me if I'd join them in a beer, and I said yes, so the whole gang of us sat around at nine-thirty in the morning drinking beer and talking about politics and the state of the city in general.

After a couple of beers, Schultz complimented me on the way I was running my campaign, especially on the Upper East Side, his area, and told me that I had made a lot of friends and was very popular. My first reaction was, "Well, that's good, because I like them."

"Well, that's fine, Walter," said Dutch. "But do you really want to be senator. Because if you do want to get elected, I'll see that the Upper East Side gives you all the votes you need. And it will only cost you five-thousand dollars."

"Dutch," I said, "I don't want to get elected that way. I've got a lot of things to do once I'm elected, and I can't afford to have any strings tying me down. If the people like me, I'd like to serve them; if they don't want me, that's all right too, but either way, I'm not going to buy an election."

Dutch laughed at me and told me everybody did it. He'd managed it for the senator before me and the one before him, and it was a simple process. All I had to do was to get a relative, a brother-in-law maybe, to bet him $5,000 that I wouldn't get elected. Dutch would bet $5,000 that I would get elected, and Dutch was not about to lose a bet. I was sure to get elected. It was as simple as that, on the surface. But no matter how you sliced it, it was buying an election, and once you buy a deal with those boys, they have something on you and you're finished as far as the gangsters are concerned.

So I thanked him a lot for being so concerned about my election but told him I thought it was bad luck to bet against myself. He said he thought I was being silly, but that was okay, if I changed my mind he'd be glad to help me out. We had a couple more rounds of beer, and after another pleasant fifteen minutes I was driven home by Tom Brown.

But I knew I was in trouble. There were 120,000 people registered to vote in that district, and 24,000 of them lived above 96th Street. No matter how much I campaigned up there, no matter how many hands I shook, babies I kissed, and overcrowded apartments I visited, I had the feeling that without Dutch I didn't have a chance. And I was right.

On Election Day I held a 20,000 majority of all the

votes cast from Greenwich Village up to 96th Street, but I lost 23,200 of the 24,000 votes cast above 96th Street, and as a result I lost the election. I knew that something was obviously wrong, because I received only 800 votes up there, and I knew that a lot more people than that were going to vote for me. I wondered what had happened to them. What had happened was quite simple: They never got the chance to vote. At five in the afternoon there were still long lines of people waiting to vote, but they couldn't get in because the voting machines were already full. Schultz had sent his people in to vote again and again. They all signed the book in green ink and with the same handwriting, and it was the damndest-looking thing you ever saw, but there it was. It could only have happened with the full connivance of the so-called Republican as well as the Democratic poll watchers, and with the cooperation of the police.

I didn't mind losing the election so much as I minded the fact that it clearly showed that the people of the city of New York were practically unfranchised. They thought they had the right to vote, but their votes were practically useless. While the people of the Upper East Side were not even able to vote, those from the rest of the district who did get to vote lost their voice because of the actions of some gangsters in the outlying sections.

The whole thing made me mad as hell, and I made up my mind to do something about it. I hired two secretaries and two notaries public, and in the evening I went out, door-to-door, and spoke to a lot of people, primarily Spanish-speaking Puerto Ricans, and got them to tell me what had happened to them on election day. The secretaries took their statements down, and

I had them signed and notarized on the spot before they could be intimidated.

It wasn't too long after I started collecting these affidavits that I noticed I was being followed by a pair of shady characters. I'd come out of my apartment house in the morning and there they'd be. They'd tail me down to my office, follow me to lunch, and at the end of the day escort me home. My business partners got a little excited about this and hired a detective to protect me, Honest Dan Costigan. He had been a truly outstanding police detective and, as his name implied, one of the most incorruptible. And as he'd just retired from the force, he was perfect for this little job.

So we'd start off in the morning, the two gangsters following me and Honest Dan following them, three cars making their way downtown to Wall Street. We'd all go to lunch together—different tables and separate checks of course—then our little parade would march back to the office. Finally I'd get my double escort home at night, and again later on, during my rounds with the secretaries and notaries on the Upper East Side. It was quite a procession, and even though the attention was at the time a little nerve-racking, I can't say it was entirely unenjoyable.

At any rate, I soon had 480 signed statements attesting to what had happened on election day. Some people had been pushed around, others forced out of the polling stations, some had had their faces slapped, and still others had had the experience of gangsters going right into the voting machine with them and voting for them. None of it made pretty reading, but it was just the sort of stuff I needed.

My first stop was the district attorney's office in New York City, but he was a Tammany Hall appointee and told me in no uncertain terms that I was wasting my time. He said that no one would be interested, and that all I would accomplish would be to get the poor people who had given the affidavits into trouble.

Next I went to Attorney General Bennett in Albany, who was also a Tammany Hall Democrat. I told him what had happened, showed him the affidavits, and said I wanted the election voided and a full investigation started. He said: "Listen, Mr. Mack, that election's over and done with, but I'll tell you what I'll do. I'll make a deal with you. You leave the affidavits with me, and the next office you want to run for, I'll guarantee you Democratic support."

Thanks, but no thanks. I seemed to be blocked at every turn, until a lawyer friend of mine told me that Franklin Roosevelt, who had just been elected President, was trying to kill Prohibition and get rid of the liquor lords and that he was willing to listen to anyone or anything that might help. I made an appointment with J. Edgar Hoover and went down to Washington to present my case. Hoover said the word had come down from Roosevelt to go after these gangsters any way he could, and this looked like as good a place as any to start, so he made an appointment for me to see the attorney for the Southern District of the State of New York, George Medalie. I went in to see Medalie, who was very impressed with the affidavits and promised to put his top assistant on the job to get these people who had signed the affidavits down before a grand jury to testify. So he pushed a button and in walked Tom Dewey, and I handed him the affidavits along with the responsibility of getting together the grand jury.

About two weeks later Dewey called asking me to come down to his office, and when I went down he said that the surprising thing about all the people whom I had convinced to sign the affidavits was that they were sticking to their stories in front of a grand jury even though they were being physically intimidated by the gangsters. They'd go home and get beaten up, but they'd still come in the next morning to testify. He congratulated me on doing a great job and said he'd like to go ahead and prosecute it on election fraud. There was, however, one condition.

I agreed, since I wanted to bring it all out into the open and clean the mess up. But what was the condition? I was to step out of the picture completely and let Dewey handle everything, including the publicity, from there on out. Fine, I said, because I just wanted the investigation started. But at the same time I thought, Why you little son of a bitch. You're not interested in doing what's right or what you ought to do. You're only interested in doing it for yourself and for what you can get out of it.

So I stepped out of the picture and Dewey started his election-fraud case. My name was never once mentioned during the investigation, but at least I got what I was after, and it eventually led to a complete cleanup of the city's election practices. Dewey went on to become famous, first as district attorney, then as governor, and finally as a two-time Republican candidate for President—a two-time loser, I'm happy to say, because I knew all the time what a selfish little rascal he was.

9

Jimmy Walker was a fine fellow and a great friend of mine, and while he was mayor of New York the city was physically in good shape. There were fewer potholes in the streets than there are now, the snow was cleared as soon as it fell, the trolleys ran on time, and there wasn't a single strike while he was around. And if corruption ran wild and everybody was on the take, well, that wasn't just in New York. Prohibition had made the entire country corrupt, and there was very little respect for the law. New York City was no different from anywhere else along that line, but unfortunately Walker happened to be mayor when somebody squealed about contract kickbacks, and he got caught with his hand in the till. No one was really surprised, since it was a common enough practice in those days—and I'd say it's still very much with us today—but there was a great moral upheaval, and the public became aroused. It takes a lot to arouse the public, but every twenty years or so they make themselves heard before they go back to sleep, and this was one of those periods.

The Republicans saw this as a great opportunity to finally elect somebody who wasn't a lackey of Tammany Hall, but since New York was, and is, a Democratic city, we wanted to run it as a combined effort rather than strictly along party lines. So we formed the Fusion Party of Democrats and Republicans, and went out to look for an honest man. We formed a committee of five and interviewed a lot of people before finally narrowing it down to two: Nathan Strauss, whose family owned WMCA Broadcasting, and Fiorello La-Guardia. We took a vote in committee and came out three to two in favor of LaGuardia as our candidate in the 1933 elections.

Although it was all before my time, the story of how LaGuardia got his start was pretty well known in local political circles. In the election of 1916, the Republicans needed somebody to run for Congress from the 3rd Assembly District, which is Manhattan's Lower East Side. It was an Irish/Italian district and solidly Democratic, so any Republican who ran didn't have a hope in hell of winning. Still, they had to put some name on the ballot, so they asked the district leader down there to come up with one. The best he could do was to recommend this little fellow who hung around the local Republican clubhouse and used to run errands for them. He was a self-taught lawyer, Italian, so he knew some of the neighbors, and it would cost the Republicans only about $1,500 to get out some circulars so that at least people would know somebody was running. The little guy they nominated was Fiorello LaGuardia. Of course he didn't have a prayer, but they got out their circulars and that was that.

LaGuardia ran hard in spite of the odds, and three days before the election the Irishman he was running against dropped dead from a heart attack. It was too late to get anybody else on the ballot, so LaGuardia won by a fluke and went down to Washington as congressman for the 3rd Assembly District. He had a great time down there and just loved it, so when he came up for reelection in 1918 he went to Frank Tanner, who was then state Republican chairman, and said he wanted to run again and he wanted to win. Tanner told him that despite his popularity there was no way he was going to get reelected, because the district was solidly Democratic and he'd only got to Congress in the first place because of a miracle. Undeterred, La-Guardia insisted there had to be a way, and Tanner, more or less jokingly, told him the only thing he could do was to resign from Congress, join the Army, get wounded, and come back a hero; then maybe there would be a chance. Well, that's exactly what LaGuardia did. He resigned, joined up, went to Europe, got shot in the leg, came back a war hero, and was reelected to Congress.

His fighting spirit was evident in Washington, and he made quite a name for himself as a champion of the underdog. His most famous piece of legislation was the Norris-LaGuardia Act, which he co-sponsored with the revered congressman George Norris of Nebraska. It helped establish labor's right to strike, picket, and conduct boycotts, and it was passed by Congress in March 1932, which made LaGuardia a name in the news when it came time for New York's municipal elections the following year.

I served as the Fusion Party's treasurer during the campaign and went out with LaGuardia on a great many of his appearances throughout the city. I never saw so much of the city as when I was running around with him. He was absolutely tireless, bursting with energy, and completely without fear. I remember that one time we were up in Harlem, which was Dutch Schultz's territory, and went up to one place where the door was guarded by a big, tough-looking hood. We tried to go past him but he blocked the entrance and told us we couldn't go in because it was a private speakeasy. With that, LaGuardia took his foot and kicked the guy in a very delicate place, saying, "Get out of my way, you bum." It was the damndest thing I ever saw. Any ordinary person would have been scared to death of getting shot, but nothing like that ever seemed to bother LaGuardia.

When we started the campaign, he said to me: "Walter, collect all the money you can, but don't spend any more than you've got. We're not going to go into debt. I don't know if we're going to be elected, but I'm not going to buy my election. I'm going to get elected if the people want me to run the city for them, and money is not going to do it, so I want you to promise me that you won't let the boys who are doing the radio and newspaper advertising spend more than we've got in the bank."

We went through that campaign spending peanuts,

because that's all we had. Towards the end, when it looked like LaGuardia was going to be elected, money finally started flowing in, but it came so late we never got around to spending it. I've been treasurer of a great many campaigns over the years, but that's the only one I know of that was actually overfunded. The cost of the whole campaign didn't run over $280,000, and we returned about 10 percent of it, some $28,000, which I think might be some sort of record.

Although it was the Fusion ticket, it could just as easily have been called the ConFusion Party, because we really didn't know what we were going to do if we managed to win, or how we would go about it. Our main goal was to break Tammany Hall's stranglehold on the city, and after we did that, we set out to clean the place up as best we could. Soon after LaGuardia was elected I went around to his new office in City Hall and he greeted me in that short, stabbing way he had of talking: "Well, Walter, what is it that *you* want?" Everybody who had worked for him wanted some sort of job in the administration, not as a handout like in the old days, but in order to help build the new order. I just looked at him for a long moment and said: "I want you to be the goddamndest mayor this city has ever seen. That's all, and that's not a lot to ask." He broke out in the broadest smile I'd ever seen, and from that moment on we were the best of friends.

I did, however, have one particular pet project I wanted him to act on right away, and that was to clean up the police department. I told him the only way he was ever going to make a decent job of being mayor was to have an honest police force behind him, and he agreed. He got a new police commissioner, and together they cleaned up the whole department. I was particularly gratified to see them indict the captain who ran the district up to 125th Street in Harlem, which was Dutch Schultz's territory. We finally proved he was in league with those gangsters, and I took great pleasure in seeing him go to jail. As far as I was concerned, that was one of the great rewards of getting involved in politics.

LaGuardia had a phobia against what he called "the political clubhouse boys," the fellows who came into politics because they didn't want to do any work. The city was full of them—was and still is today. There are people downtown right now who only come in once or twice a week and just keep on collecting their pay. And you can't fire them because they're part of the Civil Service, which is a nice name for the union of government employees. They're in every city, of course, and even the federal government is full of them, and the more seniority they get, the harder they are to get rid of. Well, LaGuardia couldn't get rid of all of them, but he cleaned house of all the part-time, well-paid opportunists and refused to hire replacements who were not qualified. Instead he got a completely independent group of people, both Republicans and Democrats, who were a top-notch bunch of administrators.

He was always, however, an extremely abrasive, dominating guy, and becoming mayor didn't soften him in the least. He loved to scream and yell, and when he got going you could hear him all the way down to Battery Park. He really got rambunctious when he didn't want to do something, and instead of arguing it out logically, he would simply pound the table and yell a lot. He was, to a certain extent, a great fraud, because he was all front; but by being louder than everyone else, he prevented others from influencing him, and if anybody crossed him, he simply fired him.

Lester Stone, who served as LaGuardia's secretary, was a nice, gentle guy with a shock of white hair. You had to have an even temper to be able to work closely with LaGuardia for very long, but Stone was dedicated to the man and his job. One day Lester called me up and said, "Walter, we're in a hell of a mess down here and you may be the only one who can straighten it out." LaGuardia hadn't been in office very long. It was in 1934–35, and the *New York Times* had already printed some unflattering articles saying he was rude, independent, and arrogant—all of which was more or less true. The mayor flew off the handle and refused to speak to anybody from the *Times*. It got to the point where a *Times* reporter wasn't even allowed into City Hall, and the subject of LaGuardia became taboo in the paper. This was a ridiculous situation and Lester knew it, but he couldn't figure a way out of it, since nobody in his right mind would try to reason with LaGuardia when he was mad. That's why Lester called me, and I went down to City Hall.

I didn't have an appointment, but I went to La-Guardia's suite of offices and stood in the archway that led into the inner sanctum. The mayor was sitting behind the big desk he worked at and was busy writing. He completely ignored me for a long time before he finally looked up at me standing there and said, "Well, Walter, what the hell do you want now."

So I went in and sat down at the desk beside him and said: "Fiorello, you're having a fight with the *Times*, and it's been going on for three or four months now, and I'm going to be frank with you. You're in the wrong, and you're behaving like a goddamn fool."

He started pounding his desk and hollering at me so that you could hear him for miles around. "Don't you talk to me like that! I won't stand for anybody talking to me like that! You can't come in here and tell me what to do!" And on and on he went. Then *I* started pounding the desk and hollering louder than he was, and the two of us went at it like a couple of fishwives. After an interminable amount of this pounding and yelling, his voice quieted down and he said to me in a normal tone, "What are you talking about?" like he had never heard me in the first place. So I explained to him how we saw the problem, that it was one of bruised ego more than anything else. We talked it out intelligently, and he eventually made it up with the *Times*. I was able to do that, where Lester Stone or one of the boys down at City Hall couldn't, because I was the only one without a job in his administration and therefore had nothing to lose. LaGuardia could fire them, but he couldn't fire me, and that was the basis of our friendship over the next twelve years. He barked an awful lot of the time, but he had a good heart, and he was trying to do a decent job.

LaGuardia and I were never close personal friends, but we liked one another enormously and he used to call on me for all sorts of odd jobs. In 1943 he asked me into his office and said there was a building the city had just taken over because of nonpayment of taxes and he had a great idea for it. It was a Shriner's Auditorium on 55th Street, a beautiful building with a big auditorium, and it seemed a shame to tear it down. He wanted me to explore the possibilities of making it into a popular-priced center for the performing arts. So I went out and did a little research and came back to him with the idea of forming an organization that would rent it from the city for one dollar a year, tax free, and turn it into a center for music and art.

He liked the idea, so I went out and collected four other people and the five of us each put in $15,000 and together formed City Center. Newbold Morris was president of the City Council at the time and did a lot of the organizing with me, and when it opened he dedicated it as "a theater for the people," which was exactly what LaGuardia had in mind. We had professionals run the theater itself, while the five of us on the board of directors were involved only to the extent that we kept the building together by raising money wherever we could. We ran it for years at a deficit, and although I retired from the board some time ago, I'm still an honorary trustee, and City Center is still running in the red. But then LaGuardia never expected it to turn a profit. His goals were above the bottom line.

When he originally came into office, the city was in bad shape because of Tammany Hall, and he said to me: "Walter, I'm going to clean up this city so that it shines. Not only the police department, but the sanitation and everything else, and to hell with the unions or anybody who stands in my way. I'm here for four years and that's it, because I'm never going to run for office again and I'd never be elected anyway, but in the four years while I'm in charge I'm going to straighten it all out and then I'm going to get lost."

LaGuardia did clean up the city and ran it like it had never been run before, but he didn't get lost after four years. He ran for two more terms and served for a total of twelve years, retiring only after he found out that he had cancer and couldn't take the rigors of another campaign. He died a few years after leaving office, but the memory of Fiorello LaGuardia lives on. He was a great politician, a civic leader, and an inspiration to municipal governments everywhere. He was honest and straightforward, fearless and tireless. He was never too worn out to hop on the back of a fire truck or to thump the street corners for a cause in which he believed. He was proud and could be disdainful of those he saw as second-rate, but was human enough to read the Sunday comics over the radio when a newspaper strike prevented their delivery to the kids he loved so much. He was a complex man and a difficult man, and he was, quite simply, the greatest mayor New York City has ever seen.

IO

"We in America today are nearer the final triumph over poverty than ever before in the history of any land." So said presidential candidate Herbert Hoover in 1928, and 58 percent of the electorate believed him. Why not? We were in a boom time, and everybody seemed to be in the chips. A lot of people at the time, and since then, have blamed the Democrats' stunning defeat that year on candidate Alfred E. Smith's Catholic religion; and, indeed, I think that was probably a major factor in his losing five of the so-called solid southern states, but as for the rest, the Republican Party was riding the crest of their own success, and Hoover was the anointed heir apparent. I don't know if anybody could have defeated Hoover that year, but the man who rode in on a wave of triumph was soon to be engulfed by that same wave when it tumbled, fast and furious, ten months after his inauguration.

The crash officially began on October 24, 1929. On that day the bottom fell out of the stock market. Overnight, $30 billion in capital disappeared as speculators were forced to sell short. Within a year national unemployment passed 4 million—out of a U.S. population of 120 million—and 1,300 banks closed, the largest being New York's Bank of the United States, with 400,000 depositors. The national income, as the gross national product was called in those days, fell from $81 billion in 1929 to $68 billion in 1930. It would eventually slide down to $40 billion before 1932. Unemployment doubled each year, up to 8 million in 1931 and an estimated 17 million by 1932. Within two years of the start of the crash, over 2,500 banks had closed, taking their depositors' money with them, and the financial crisis claimed responsibility for 21,000 suicides. By 1932, 34 million Americans had no income at all, and the "triumph over poverty" that Hoover had foreseen just a few years previously had disappeared as the boom bubble burst.

Again, although Hoover was not personally responsible for the Depression, he could have controlled it and lessened its total impact. As it was, he did nothing of note, which was the worst thing of all. His great belief in "the American system of rugged individualism" got completely out of hand, but it had nothing to do with my Republican Party. I'm convinced that if it hadn't been for Franklin Roosevelt getting into office and giving way and helping the people out of the depths they were in, we would have had a very bloody revolution in this country. Roosevelt took a lot of steps immediately, and a lot of them were suspect—in fact many were downright illegal—but he did *something*. He was positive and he turned the country around. It took us until the end of the thirties to pull completely out of the Depression, and by then we were gearing up for a war, which, as horrible as that might have been, was nevertheless a boost to the economy. But Roosevelt's election was the light at the end of a very dark tunnel, although there were many, especially on Wall Street and in the business community, who never saw it that way. That, I think, was their own blindness. Personally, I did very well during the Depression; in fact, I prospered more than I ever had before. When all my friends were making hundred of thousands on paper every day, I was still peddling along in the textile business, making one day's pay after another just to keep my head above water. Then, when I was at Chain & General Equities, we were building a small but solid base in a field that would actually grow during a depressed economy. We dealt with grocery stores, which went through the Depression relatively unscathed; we were in good shape because, no matter what, people had to eat, and they went to the stores where they could buy things the cheapest, like Safeway, Krogers, and some of the chains that were just forming and in which we were investing. And unlike everybody else, we didn't own anything on margin, so we weren't overextended.

As the value of money declined sharply, the people who lost most were those who had everything on margin. They were wiped out, but we were in a different situation. Let's say we had a thousand shares of Kroger Grocery Stores; even though the price of Kroger went from $50 a share in 1928 down to $10 in 1930, you still owned it as long as you didn't owe money on it and weren't forced to sell. And we didn't owe so we didn't sell, and we rode it out okay. After all, the stores were the same, the management was the same, and they were selling to the same people, even if the value of money was less. So if you didn't have to sell short, which we didn't, nothing really changed.

Of course, a lot of our investors did sell on the open market, which was entirely up to them; there was nothing to stop them from doing that; but as a company, Chain & General Equities stayed in good shape. I went through that period much more comfortably than most of my friends who had been speculating—making $50,000 one day and $25,000 the next—because they had nothing but paper money. I didn't have many friends who cracked and jumped, but I did have a lot who were in very bad shape and went absolutely broke.

It was during the initial depths of the Depression, the time when none of us thought it could get any worse—though, in fact, it would get worse—that David Milton first approached me. He was the son-in-law of John D. Rockefeller—he'd married Abby Rockefeller, John D.'s only daughter—and had formed a company called Equity Corporation that dealt with equity securities. Whereas I specialized in chain stores, they specialized in any old thing, and they got themselves in a lot of trouble. At the time, Milton had some great theorists and chart readers working for him, but they didn't know how to read a chart or work out a theory,

because everything they did was wrong. The Rocke-
fellers had put about $25 million into this corporation
and they still weren't doing very well. David Milton
had seen my record running Chain & General and
asked me if I'd come over and help them straighten
out Equity Corporation.

I told him I had my hands full and sort of ducked
the issue, but soon after that David Milton made a
deal to buy Chain & General for cash and merge it into
Equity Corporation. Part of the deal was that I would
go over to Equity as vice-president of the newly combined corporation and straighten out their situation.
When we were fully merged, Equity Corporation stood
as an open trust with assets of around $50 million. Most
investment trusts at the time were limited by their
charters and bylaws both as to the size of the investments they could make and the fields in which they
could invest, but an open trust has no restrictions
whatsoever on the use of its money, and $50 million
was a great deal of money at that time for an open
trust.

At about that same time, 1932–33, another fellow
who had also been watching my record came to see me.
His name was Wallace Groves, and he also wanted to
go into the investment business, but all he had was
money. Prince & Whitely Trading Company was an investment trust that had gone bankrupt by speculating
heavily and was trading its stock at the time for around
50¢ a share. Groves said he wanted to buy control of
Prince & Whitely and then rebuild it as an entirely new
company, and he wanted me to go out on the market
and buy the control for him.

This intrigued me, because here was a man who was

willing to back me with all the money I needed, and who, if we managed to get control, wanted to rebuild. It was a tremendous opportunity, and I told him that I would help him; but since we had to buy the stock on the open marketplace, we had to be careful because otherwise people would know that we were buying it up and that would run the price up. The way to handle it was to buy a bit and then sell a bit through a variety of brokers and fronts until eventually we had enough. Now that wasn't exactly standard practice, but with a lot of money to play with, it was a good way to camouflage what we were doing. Groves agreed to put into the bank all the money I needed so that it could be drawn on at any time.

This was to be an early example of the mammoth takeovers that are common practice today, and have been in every depression/recession since the thirties. It is during these times of tight money that investors are afraid of the securities of a company in trouble, which means that the company's stock values go below their real net worth, or their replacement cost. That's the time to try to get control on the market at a discount. Prince & Whitely was just such a company, and all I had to do was to deliver the stock.

Since the stock was going at the time for 50¢, I didn't know what I was finally going to have to pay for it all, but I said I'd try to keep it under a buck, which seemed pretty reasonable. I got together with a good friend of mine on Wall Street, Chauncy Wardell, who was married to the daughter of Chief Justice Charles Evans Hughes, and together, over a period of time we bought 65 percent of the outstanding shares of Prince & Whitely at an average of 75¢ a share. The whole thing cost Groves about $750,000, a lot of money back then, and all he got for it was a bankrupt company that owned a bunch of stocks but owed more money than those stocks were worth.

Groves asked me if I'd work out a plan of reorganization to take the company out of bankruptcy. I did that, and he settled with the creditors and used Prince & Whitely as a shell, a corporation trading on the American Exchange, with a number of public stockholders but without any specific business or real assets, and thus flexible enough to invest as it saw fit. Then he came over to me and asked me to help him run Prince & Whitely. I told him that I already had a job and wasn't interested in moving just to buy and sell securities again. I was really only interested in reorganizing and rebuilding companies. Trading was what had gotten Prince & Whitely into trouble before, and if that's what he intended to go on doing, I didn't want any part of it. All I really wanted to do was to reorganize and rebuild.

Fine, he said, because that's what he was interested in doing also: liquidating all the securities and taking that money to explore special situations. He proposed that he become chairman of the board and I become president, and that we change the name of the firm from Prince & Whitely to Phoenix Securities Company, after the phoenix, the legendary bird that grows out of its own ashes. Since we intended to create new companies out of old ashes it seemed appropriate. It was also prophetic.

Actually, I didn't know Wallace all that well at the time. I tried to check him out and found out that he came from Chicago, had gone to Georgetown University, and that his money came from Canada, but that's about all I could find out. He seemed like a nice fellow, and he certainly was smart, but still it worried me to go into a situation like that so blindly, so I said to him: "I'll tell you what I'll do. I'll agree to come in and help run Phoenix as president in special situations, if you'll agree, because you own the company and you're the largest stockholder, that if I say no to a deal, you won't go into it. In other words, I have a negative vote, but I won't be negative unless I have a damn good reason."

To my astonishment, he said: "Fine. Let's shake on it," and that was our deal. There was never anything in writing, but he lived up to every word of it. He was a great man for living up to his word, which really was his bond. Years later he said to me, "If you have to put something in writing, then I'll find you ten lawyers who'll find a way of getting around it, but if you shake hands with a man and he gives you his word, then there's no way he can get around it." Legally, perhaps, that doesn't stand, but with Wallace Groves it was better than any law.

I went to David Milton before I made my deal with Wallace and told him that I wanted to leave Equity Corporation because all they were really doing was fiddling around with securities, which was not my strength. My expertise was in chain stores, not as a trader in general securities. I told him about Wallace, and that Phoenix had the possibility of building a great future, but David made quite a fuss. He didn't want to lose me, so we worked out a deal whereby I would spend my mornings with David at Equity, which was at 48 Wall Street on the south side of the street, and my afternoons across the street at Phoenix, which was at 49 Wall Street. It wasn't all that confusing, because Equity was working in general securities while Phoenix was specializing in buying control of companies that were in financial trouble but that could be reorganized and rebuilt through new management and an infusion of working capital. But I couldn't do justice to either one, so finally I left Equity and went over to spend my full time with Phoenix and Wallace Groves.

Wallace was a very shy, quiet sort of guy, but he had the best business intuition of anybody I've ever run across. He never took an active part in the running of Phoenix—he always had a lot of dealings of his own on the outside—but he and I would confer over the problems and work out a solution on most things. Then, when we went into negotiations, he would let me do all the talking, all the bargaining, while he wouldn't say a word. Every once in a while, though, he'd send me little pieces of paper on which he'd written something like, "They're thinking a million and a quarter and that's as far as they'll go," and invariably he was right. He'd just sit there and watch what was going on and let his intuition take over, and he had the damndest judgment I ever saw.

But he never wanted to get involved in anything out in front or in the public eye. All the time I was with him at Phoenix I remained active in politics, and one day Newbold Morris, a good friend of mine who was then the head of the trustees of the Metropolitan Opera, came to me and said that they were in a bit of trouble for cash and could I lay my hands on $50,000 for them. This was in 1937, and by then we were in great shape, with Phoenix having made a lot of money, so I was a natural person to come to as a source since I knew whom we had made money for. I was active in the public eye but really didn't have any money, while Wallace was just the opposite, and I thought this might be a good opportunity to get him involved. So I told Morris that if he could get his board of directors to agree to elect Wallace to the board, I thought I could get him to make a $50,000 charitable contribution. I realize now that it was a hell of a lot to ask, but Morris said he'd see what he could do.

A couple of weeks later he came back to me and said, okay, they'd found a vacancy on the board and he could guarantee Wallace's election, so I went right in to see Wallace and I said: "Wallace, I've got a hell of an idea for you. You're not involved in anything outside, and I know that the board of trustees of the Metropolitan Opera is extremely well looked up to, and I think that if you made a contribution of, well, let's say something around $50,000, I can probably get you made a member of the board."

He said he wanted to sleep on it, and the following morning at nine he came in, sat down in my office, and said that he'd thought about it all the night before and the answer was that he wasn't really interested. However, he handed me a check for $50,000 made out to the Met. That's the sort of person he was.

Wallace and I had a wonderful and profitable number of years at Phoenix, and when we finally liquidated the company he ended up with about $30 million for the sale of his stock. It was, after all, mostly all his, and even though he could easily have retired, he went on to do other things. He had always been interested in natural resources, developing land, that sort of thing, and he went down to Southern California, near the Mexican border along the Rio Grande, and bought a lot of land. He planted orange groves, developed farms, and created life out of what had previously been desert. And, of course, he made a fortune.

His biggest project, though, occured in the late forties when he bought Grand Bahama Island from the government of Nassau. It was a big island and full of lumber, but nobody could get to it because of all the coral reefs that surrounded it. But then, nothing like that ever stopped Wallace. He came back to the States and bought a lot of Army amphibious ducks—troop carriers that were used during the war to cross lakes, swamps, and rivers and that were as home on land as they were in the water. Taking a tip from the Army, Wallace used them to crawl right up over the coral reefs and onto the land. He lumbered the entire island, sold the lumber to England, and made another fortune. Once he had cleared the island, he renamed it Freeport, dug harbors, and developed it. Then he sold it off bit by bit. All told he made about $500 million out of his Bahamian venture.

Soon after he took over the island, he asked me to come down and stay with him. He sent his private seaplane over to Palm Beach to pick me up, and we flew to his place on Little Cat Cay. He had built a magnificent stone house there, and life was truly luxurious. All we had to do was swim and fish and eat too much. We got up in the morning, had a big breakfast, swam and then went fishing, came back and ate too much for lunch, then went for a swim and went fishing again until it was time for dinner, where we again ate too much. Well, after about three or four days of that I didn't know what was happening in the rest of the world, but I knew I was fed up with fishing. You could catch all the fish you wanted in the first fifteen minutes, so what was the point.

On about the fourth night of this, he and I were playing backgammon and he said: "You know, Walter, you and I have done a lot of things together, and I'd like to go back into partnership with you. I need somebody like you to help me out down here. The lumbering is going along just fine, and after that I want to develop the whole island and I'd like you to do it with me. If you'll come down here and spend five years with me, I'll build you a beautiful house on the tail end of Little Cat Cay and pay you $400,000 a year tax free."

Now that was a hell of a nice offer, and I didn't want to insult the guy since he was a friend of mine, but I couldn't live that life for all the money in the world. I'd go nuts. So I told him I'd think it over and let him know as soon as I got back to New York. I couldn't wait to get home—just two weeks of the good life down there was driving me crazy—and I wrote him a nice letter telling him that because of my family ties up north, I couldn't accept his offer. Wallace and I have remained good friends over the years, but his generous offer was one I've never had any regrets about refusing.

II

After we liquidated all of the securities Phoenix held, Wallace Groves and I had about $800,000 in cash, so we went on the prowl looking for companies to reorganize. Since this was 1933—the depth of the Depression—there was no shortage of corporations in trouble. The first one we got involved with was Celotex, a wallboard business that had gone into bankruptcy.

The famous Celotex board was made from the remains of sugarcane, a byproduct known as bagasse. The process is to squeeze the sap out of the bagasse, which is then ground up, put through a shredder, washed, mixed with chemicals and then finally with cement and plaster. This is then pressed into a strong wallboard. It was an excellent product; the chemicals prevented insects from breeding in it, and it was insulated, the first insulated board in this country. The only reason the company was in trouble was that it couldn't get its raw material, the bagasse, on a regular guaranteed basis. They were completely at the mercy of the sugar growers who were mostly in Cuba.

Wallace and I studied Celotex and decided that it had a future, since it was a cheap way to make a very good board, but that we would have to find some way to make sure we got our raw material. We put through our plan for reorganization and, using $500,000 of Phoenix's money, bought control of Celotex and went to work trying to straighten it out. I became chairman of the board, and the first thing I did was to go down to Louisiana, where I bought the largest sugar plantation in the state, the South Coast Corporation, 40,000 acres in all. We weren't particularly interested in going into the sugar business, we were just trying to insure a regular supply of bagasse; but soon we were doing so well that we had a surplus and could sell bagasse as well as sugar on the open market, and in no time we were making quite a bit of money. What had started out as incidental to Celotex's wallboard became a good source of income.

The good Lord has always been very good to me, and once more luck came my way—again through the back door. Within a year after we took over Celotex, the head of the Pan American Petroleum Corporation came over to us and said that they'd been doing some shooting of electrical depth charges into the earth's surface across our sugar plantation in order to locate gas and oil fields, and they thought that we might have something down under there. He asked if they could take out a lease and do some exploring. We agreed, they drilled a few wells, and before long we were making more money out of oil than we ever had out of wallboard, sugar, or bagasse. It was just a case of pure dumb luck. By then Celotex was well out of the red and doing very nicely, and when we finally sold it in 1935, we made a profit of $2 million. Not a bad start for a new company.

Celotex established the modus operandi of Phoenix. We would find a company in trouble, investigate its weaknesses, and if we could solve its problems, we would buy in, provide new capital, and fix up its management. I would go on the board of the new company, and that way I'd be in a position to reorganize the firm. All of this time I was, in essence, an employee of Phoenix, with a salary of around $60–65,000 a year; but of course I had some stock in Phoenix, and as it grew my stock became more valuable. But Wallace was actually the person who profited the most, since he owned almost all the stock himself. When I first bought it for him at around 75¢ a share, he told me that I could buy as much as I wanted at exactly the price he'd paid for it, a generous offer indeed, since he'd taken all the chances, but unfortunately I didn't have much money in those days, so my purchase was minimal. If I had been able to buy back in the early days, I would have been a multimillionaire many times over by the time we liquidated towards the end of the decade, but simply making a pile of money for myself has never been one of my prime goals. To build, to work, and to enjoy life have always been much more important.

We took on a lot of companies around this time (that is, of course, provided that they had a viable product in the first place), but basically there were always two things wrong with all of them: lousy management and lack of control. If we did make a decision to go into a company, we'd clean them up and run them efficiently until they showed a profit, and then sell them. Our primary rule before ever going in, though, was to get controlling interest, because without that you're just another stockholder and you haven't got the power to do what you want.

Between 1935 and 1937 we worked with a lot of companies; dealing with one didn't stop us from going into another. For instance, we were running the National Brass & Copper Company when one of our most interesting ventures came along. United Cigars—Whelan Stores, which turned out to be a $22 million operation in the end, were the country's largest dealers in cigarettes, but they went into bankruptcy for a number of reasons that soon became apparent to us. They had over a hundred cigar stores in New York City, and they were a big, big company, yet their stock was selling on the market for only around 50¢ a share. It seemed to me that these stores would provide an enormous, ready-made retail outlet for anything we wanted to sell, so why were they in trouble? The simple answer was that they got into a lot of trouble over a bunch of bad leases. They had two kinds of stores, those in high-traffic locations, such as the 42nd or 34th Street areas, and the others in outlying or off-the-beaten-track areas of the city; but they all had the same kind of deal. They would only pay so much rent no matter where they were, but they would always include a percentage of the profits to the landlord in those deals. What this meant, basically, was that when the store was in a good location it made a lot of money for everybody, and especially the landlord, but when the store was a loser it didn't make anything for the company just because of the low rent. Fair enough, except that all the stores in the high-profit areas were owned by George Whelan himself, the sole owner of Whelan Drugs and his own landlord, so while he made a lot of money, his company lost as much. He had two things going for him at the same time: Where the store was a winner, it was his; where it was a loser, the company absorbed the loss. Today that sort of operation is, of course, illegal, but back then anything went.

Well, Whelan wanted to get out anyway, so we bought his shares—but he kept the leases on his stores— and took control of the company. The first thing we did was to go into bankruptcy court to get out of all those bad leases, including Whelan's. Then we set out to rebuild the entire structure of the stores, which turned out to be a long-drawn-out process, a siege really, that lasted a couple of years.

At about the same time we learned that the Hahn Department Store chain was in deep trouble despite the fact that they owned a number of terrific stores, including Jordan Marsh in Boston and C. B. Harvey in Cincinnati. Their stock had dropped from $57 a share in 1929 to around a dollar by 1932. The more I studied their case, the more it became obvious that it was all a result of bad management.

There was a clause in their bylaws that stated that if four dividend periods passed without payment, the owners of preferred stock had the right to elect 51 percent of the board of directors, so I went out and secretly bought as much of the preferred as I could lay my hands on. I didn't want anyone to know what I was doing, so I bought through various houses and kept the stock in the name of the different brokerage firms —thus it was Merrill, Lynch or Reynolds & Company or whoever who owned the stock, not Phoenix—until about two months before the election of the board of directors, when I had it all transferred to our name. By then, of course, we already had control of the stock.

One of the biggest holders of both common and preferred stock in Hahn was the brokerage firm of Lehman Brothers, and as soon as they discovered what I had done, Philip Lehman, one of the senior partners, called me on the telephone. He said that he understood we owned a fair share of preferred (by that time it was about 53 percent), and did I realize that preferred owners had the right to elect the majority of the company's directors. I answered that I had heard a rumor to that effect, but as yet I didn't know what I was going to do about it, which was not exactly the whole truth. He then went on to say that he'd very much like it if I would vote with him on the members of the board. I told him I'd let him know and kept him on the hot seat until about two weeks before the fatal day when we made a deal whereby we would each elect the same number of directors but that I would go in as chairman of the finance committee with the power to reorganize.

The first thing we did after we had control was to

rename the organization Allied Department Stores and put in Earl Puckett, a hell of a good guy, as president. Not only was he young and bright but he was an accountant, and that's exactly what we needed, because without inventory controls in a store you'll lose your shirt, and Puckett was a great man with a pencil.

I've been in a lot of businesses in my life, but the department store business is the toughest in the world. For instance, when I first went into Jordan Marsh to do a study of it as our biggest and most important store, I went into the dress department and there were probably twenty different sizes and eight different colors of the same item. Then there would be other variations in cloth, texture, and weight, and all of those would have to be changed four or five times a year depending on the season. Then, in the ladies' shoe department there were forty different kinds of shoes in twelve different sizes, and it was all a matter of guessing as to style each season. With that kind of situation, unless you have exact inventory control, you've got a hell of a mess on your hands. Earl Puckett established such detailed inventory reports and control that the entire business began to turn around almost immediately.

In all the businesses Phoenix went into during the thirties, our job was to smooth out the financial problems and straighten up management without ever running the actual business itself. That was left to the best professionals we could get, but by making a thorough study of the business and getting to know how it operated, I was able to pinpoint problems on the financial side. When we first started out with Allied, I found a lot of things that had been done that simply had no right to be done, and I just laid down the law. For instance, one of the regulations that the previous board of directors had put through required that we get the approval of Lehman Brothers before making any further acquisition. This meant that Allied could not purchase any new stores without the nod from the brokerage house that controlled the board before we came along. And for giving this approval, Lehman Brothers got a flat 3 percent of the purchase price. Well, I canceled that immediately, and when they came to me squawking I simply told them that we were going to buy new stores as we wished and we weren't going to pay them a dime unless we used their services, which we never did. It didn't make me very popular at Lehman Brothers, but that didn't bother me in the least.

Another thing I found out was that all our insurance —and there was a lot of it, because these stores carried enormous inventories—was with one company, and that company was owned by Lehman Brothers. Again, it was a rule that had been passed by the previous board of directors, and again it didn't make any sense. I immediately canceled it and opened the bidding to other insurance companies. Again Lehman Brokers came to me and said I couldn't do it. But I went ahead, and I told them that if they didn't like it they could sue me.

Lehman Brothers never did sue me, because the stores were by then prospering very nicely, but they did want to get rid of me in the worst way, so I made a deal to convert our preferred stock into so many shares of common, which we then sold off in the open market. Lehman Brothers helped us to sell the stock— they were more than glad to see us on our way—and we came out of it with about $2.5 million in profit, which was pretty good for a two-year involvement.

We were very lucky that we were able to straighten out every company we went into and make money before selling it back to the public. Phoenix was getting quite a good name for itself, and companies that found themselves in trouble were beginning to come to us for help. One of them was Autocar, a big automobile and truck building plant based in Ardmore, Pennsylvania. Autocar had been around since the turn of the century, but they got themselves in a lot of financial trouble and came to me to see if I could reorganize them. I went in as chairman of the board and set out to learn as much as I could about the trucking business, which was very different from the automobile business. Whereas the latter was entirely an assembly-line process, the trucking business was a hand-made operation. Everything was on special order, so instead of turning out a line of three hundred or so Fords or Chevrolets a day, Autocar was able to turn out only five or six on special order. It was all very expensive and wasteful.

I've always been a sort of pioneer, ready to try new things and eager to experiment with new solutions, and I wanted to do something for the trucking industry as well as for Autocar, so I hired Raymond Lowey, the famous industrial designer, to see if he could streamline the product. I really wanted a new kind of truck, one that could be standardized and produced more efficiently. Lowey made a study of the entire problem and came up with a brilliant solution: He noted that we were wasting a lot of space and material with the engine sticking out in front, so he designed a cab over the engine that eliminated a lot of the waste and at the same time improved visibility. It started an entirely new trend in the design and manufacture of trucks, and Autocar was there first. It also helped take the company out of bankruptcy, and when we sold out of Autocar, we made a nice profit.

Another company that came to us for help was Certain-Teed Products, a big manufacturer of roofing materials. The president came in to see me. They were going downhill fast and he didn't know why, so he asked that I come in and help him reorganize in the same way that I had done for so many other companies. I agreed to study the problem for him, so I spent about two weeks going through his business, and it was clear to me that his only problem was that he had no management. His son-in-law was sales manager, but he would come in at around ten in the morning and then leave about three in the afternoon to play golf. His uncle was his accountant; his son, his cousin, and half a dozen others were also on the books as employees, and none of them seemed to be doing much of anything.

So I went back to the president and said, "I don't think you really want me and I don't think I want to go into your business because, number one, you're going to have to fire all your executives and they're all your relatives, and number two, I wouldn't touch it unless I had complete control to do as I saw fit."

He thanked me very much for the advice and left, and I thought that was the end of it, but about two months later he called me up and asked to see me again. We met, and he offered to sell me complete control so that I could do what I needed to save his company. Well, I went in there and I did what he couldn't do: I fired all his relatives, cleaned house, and set the entire company on its feet. It was a good business to begin with, but it was just wilting away through lack of attention, so I worked hard getting the job done.

I got to the point where I could walk through a factory and tell whether or not that factory was operating satisfactorily just by the tempo of the men, their atttiude, what they were doing, and how enthusiastic they were about their work. You get the feel and the smell of the place right away, and that goes for any business. Certain-Teed was no exception. Its problems were fairly obvious once I got in there, and I'd say the whole job didn't take longer than nine months.

During the middle thirties, Phoenix Securities had the record of being the fastest-growing investment company in the United States, and for me it was enormous fun running it. With each individual acquisition, Wallace Groves helped out during the preliminary negotiations, particularly when we were buying not on the open market but directly from the owners, which is when the bargaining table is all-important and where Groves was all-knowing; but once the deal was made, I had a free hand while he just stayed in the background.

In 1934 I went to Europe for a month's vacation. I was sailing on the *Queen Elizabeth*, and just before I left Wallace came to me and said that a great friend of his mother's would also be on board. His name was Ernest Woodruff, and Wallace thought that we ought to get to know one another, so he went along with me to the ship to introduce us.

Ernest Woodruff had headed a group of investors that bought the Coca-Cola Company in 1919 for $25

111

million; four years later he turned the company over to his son, Robert, who was then thirty-three. By 1934 Coca-Cola was not only the world's largest soft drink company, but it so dominated the market that it was, in effect the only game around. At the time, I had no idea that I would one day be involved in a head-on collision with them when I took over Pepsi—that was still four years away, and it was the last thing on my mind—but since both father and son, Ernest and Robert, would be on the crossing with their wives it was logical that we get together.

The first day out I was in the bar having a drink when Ernest Woodruff came in and sat down alongside me. He started talking about Wallace, and he seemed to know a lot about him. Apparently he had gone to school with Wallace's mother down in Atlanta and had once been more than a little fond of her. We talked for quite a while, and soon after Robert came in—he was only five years older than me, so we had more in common than I did with his father—and we all had a couple of drinks and a nice chat. After a bit I said that I was going to buy into the ship's pool that night. I mentioned that I had been a navigational officer running the Atlantic during the war and that I thought I could pretty well judge what kind of distance the ship would make over night. I said I'd just been up on the bridge and that a stiff head wind was blowing, and since we were due to pass the banks of Nova Scotia during the night I thought it would probably turn into quite a gale; so my guess was that we wouldn't make very good time and a low pool was the best bet. Robert said that I should know about these things and he wanted to buy in with me, and the old man said he'd like to go in too. So I went out and bought a low pool, which won, and we collected about $1,200, split three ways.

The next night we were again having our drink together in the lounge, and we talked about what we were going to bet that night. I said that I thought that we were picking up steam to try to make up for the losses of the day before, so I intended to buy in the top range. They both went along with me, and again we won. But the third night when we got together the old man said, "You've fooled me twice, young fellow, and you've been lucky, but from here on out I'm going to keep my winnings." Robert went in with me, but the old man had been the smart one. We lost all our winnings on that third try and kept right on losing the rest of the pools until we reached Britain. There we all parted friends, Robert and I slightly poorer than when we started out, while Ernest had a nice piece of change to add to his already considerable fortune.

III

The Years with Pepsi-Cola

12

Late in 1936 a fellow by the name of James Carkner came in to see me. He was president of Loft, Inc., which operated a chain of 115 candy stores, and he was in financial trouble. First he went to the Marine Midland Bank to try to float a loan. After looking over his financial statements they said they couldn't do anything, but they suggested he try me. His problems were twofold: One, he couldn't meet his payroll; and two, he was involved in a lawsuit with one of his principal stockholders, Charles Guth, who also happened to be his predecessor as president of Loft, Inc.

I told Carkner I didn't know anything about the candy business but that I'd investigate it and get back to him in a week—if he could wait that long. He could and would, so we went over to their factory in Queens, and it struck me that with all of the candy they were making it would be a good source for providing nickel candy bars to our United Cigar–Whelan Drug outlets.

The Loft factories were also making a syrup for a drink called Pepsi-Cola which they sold at their candy-store soda fountains, but at first this wasn't of as much interest to me as the candy manufacture itself. The big profit in the candy business was in nickel bars, so I agreed to loan them $400,000 convertible at my option to common stock at 50¢ a share. This got them out of the first jam, the payroll; but the second, the lawsuit, was far more complicated, and it concerned that second product they were manufacturing in Queens—Pepsi-Cola. Back in 1893, Caleb Bradham, a druggist, from New Bern, North Carolina, had started experimenting with ground kola nuts from Africa, which he first brewed into a tea, then added sugar, seltzer, and pepsin, and turned it into a stomach tonic. He called it Pepsin Cola. By 1902 it had done so well that he founded a company called Pepsi-Cola, shifted away from the pepsin–stomach tonic image, and marketed it as a soft drink. Bradham left the drug-store business to devote himself full-time to the new drink, and within a year he was producing 8,000 gallons of the syrup. Within five years he was up to over 100,000 gallons and had established a network of forty bottling plants. Everything was going along fine until the sugar glut of 1920, when the world price of sugar dropped from 30¢ a pound in August to 8¢ in December. Caleb Bradham had bought tons of it for his drink at 22¢ and lost $150,000 in one year, which forced him into bankruptcy. He went through two reorganizations and three other bankruptcies and in 1931 went into a liquidation sale in Richmond, Virginia. Enter Charles Guth.

Guth had been president of Loft since 1930, and one of the store operations that bothered him was the soda counter. A tremendous amount of Coca-Cola was sold over Loft's counters, so Guth went to Coke and told them that since his stores used so much of their product he should get a volume discount. Coca-Cola has always been arbitrary as hell, and they told him to go whistle, which naturally didn't sit too well with him; so he set out to acquire his own cola drink. He went to the bankruptcy sale in Richmond and bought the formula, trademark, and goodwill of Pepsi for $14,000. They had some awfully good food chemists over at Loft back then, so Guth gave them the formula, and one of those chemists, Tom Elmezzi, rearranged it, dropping the pepsin along the way, and produced the Pepsi-Cola formula as it is today.

At first Pepsi was sold exclusively at Loft's counters, but in 1932 Guth branched out into the bottling business, and two years later left Loft to look after Pepsi full-time; but he left taking along 91 percent of Pepsi's stock. When James Carkner succeeded him as president of the candy company he naturally assumed that Pepsi belonged to Loft, since Guth had used Loft's cash reserves to buy it in the first place, and so he sued Guth for the return of Pepsi's stock to the company. Guth, however, also owned a great deal of Loft stock, and Carkner was afraid that Guth would gather enough votes at the next stockholders' meeting to oust him as president and thus the suit would be dropped. But, by converting some of the debt to Phoenix into shares, we were able to avert this by holding enough shares and proxies to control that next stockholders' meeting. I was elected to Loft's board of directors along with three others from Phoenix, and the suit against Guth pressed on.

The case was argued in Wilmington, Delaware, where Pepsi-Cola was registered; on September 17, 1938, the chancellor of Delaware handed down a decision giving Loft Guth's 91 percent of Pepsi's shares. It was a clear case of corporate opportunity. Not only had Guth used company money to buy Pepsi for Loft's fountain use, but I was told that he had a meeting of the board just before I got into the picture and at a New Year's Eve party got them all drunk and had them pass a resolution giving the Pepsi business to him. He immediately appealed the decision and, pending the outcome, the chancellor decreed that Pepsi was to be governed by a board of seven directors—three of ours, three of Guth's, and a seventh to be chosen by a unanimous vote. I became president of the company and Guth the general manager. It was a complicated arrangement that was to last for the next six months, because it was like a two-headed monster trying to function while in constant battle with itself. We couldn't agree on anything, and Guth, in his position as general manager, went out of his way to make life more than just a little difficult for me.

I remember my first day in the office at Pepsi's plant in Long Island City. It was a chilly day in October, but I was far from chilly. The general manager, Mr. Guth, had assigned the president, me, to an office which was a cubbyhole directly above the boiler room. I looked around the space, which didn't take very long, and there was nothing there. No paper, no pencils, no nothing. I called my secretary and said I wanted some office tools so that I could start working, and she said she was sorry but that Pepsi employees had been instructed by the general manager not to supply us with anything, since there wasn't anything in the court order requiring them to give me a pencil. A little later in the day I wanted to go to the men's room but it was locked, and I was told that only Mr. Guth had the key, which he handed out personally to whomever he saw fit. Well, I knew that was hopeless, so I found a little restaurant around the corner and used their john for the next six months.

But if the situation at the Pepsi plant was impossible, board meetings were even more so. The six of us could never agree on anything, no matter how inconsequential, so naturally there was no way we'd ever elect a seventh member to that board. The chancellor, who had saddled us with this impossible situation, came to the rescue when he appointed Arthur T. Vanderbilt as the seventh member. Vanderbilt was a professor of law at New York University and chairman of the National Committee on Traffic Law Enforcement, a qualification tailor-made for our boardroom gridlock.

I tried not to let any of this bother me, since I had a job to do in straightening out this company. I suspected Guth was no good and that he was simply out to steal a company, so I went about my business, brought in my own pencils, and made my regular trips to the restaurant around the corner. At last, in April 1939, the appeal was denied and Guth was out. He left with the Pepsi franchise in the Baltimore area, which he had set up with his own money and to which he was entitled, but we were rid of him and we could get on with reorganization.

When I first became involved with Loft, Pepsi was not even a serious consideration. I was in there to re-structure the candy company, and I tried to turn its concentration towards the money-maker, the nickel candy bar that would then feed our own United Cigar–Whelan Stores. And I wasn't even too sure that Loft would ever win its suit against Guth. Others, however, contended at the time that we at Phoenix had agreed to help Loft out simply because of the Pepsi tangle—Pepsi after all did turn a profit of $2 million in 1936—but this was entirely untrue. That didn't convince some of Loft's stockholders, however, and they sued the company, as well as Phoenix, in December 1938, stating that we had known all the time that Pepsi-Cola was a valuable franchise and that I had taken an illegal advantage of the situation by lending the original $400,000 with the knowledge that the convertible common stock would be worth a great deal more when Loft won their case. And indeed, when the first verdict came down in September 1938, Loft's stock jumped from $2 to $5 a share overnight. We *did* convert our outstanding debt into shares at a much lower price and thus made in the neighborhood of $4 million profit on our investment, which by then had passed the million-dollar mark. But this was really incidental. It was just another case of blind luck.

That particular suit was argued in the courts for months, and just dragged on and on; and all it really was was a strike suit, brought without merit, for the primary purpose of making enough trouble so that an advantageous settlement could be made out of court.

Anybody could have bought the stock when we bought it, because it was on the open market and worthless, but we were being penalized. Finally my lawyers came to me and said, "Look, let's make a settlement by taking money out of one pocket and putting it into another, from Phoenix to Loft; and since Phoenix owns so much stock in Loft, everybody will benefit." I suppose that made sense, but it was the lawyers for the other side who really bothered me. All they were after was their fee. They were strike lawyers, plain and simple. So Phoenix paid a million dollars in cash to Loft, but since we already owned nearly half the company anyway, we'd be getting back that half while the other half would be working capital that Loft needed and Phoenix could afford. And as for the lawyers for the other side, they got an $80,000 fee, the biggest they'd ever seen, and I think a hell of a lot of money for a firm that was involved in many stockholders' strike suits. The firm, by the way, was Javits & Javits; and although the older brother, Ben, was the chief instigator, the younger one, Jacob, was of the same school. Jake, of course, went on to become the revered senator from New York, but to this day when I see him, I know he remembers what I told him I thought of him back then. He is, as I am, a liberal Republican, so our paths have crossed frequently over the past forty years, but neither of us will ever forget our first bitter meeting in December 1938.

Once these initial lawsuits were out of the way and it looked like we could focus on business, I started studying the soft drink industry, and particularly the colas. I was (and still am) a great one for trying to find out the history and fundamentals of a company so that I could know what happened to it, what made it grow, and what made it get into trouble. Loft's problems were again bad management, as well as a concentration on fancy candies instead of the money spinner, the nickel bar, and so their problems didn't interest me all that much. The story of Pepsi-Cola and the entire soft drink market, however, quickly became a fascinating one—at least for me.

Back in the middle of the nineteenth century, when the English were opening up the interior of Africa, they came across a tribe that had the greatest endurance for carrying heavy packs long distances over the mountains. The men of this tribe carried a little sack on their hip which contained something that looked like a chestnut, a green chestnut, that they chewed all the time. This was the kola, or cola, nut, and it was prized by the natives as a water purifier, love potion, and hangover cure in addition to being an energizer. Some of the nuts made it back to England, where a chemist studied its effects and wrote up his report in an international druggists' journal.

John S. Pemberton, a druggist from Atlanta, Georgia, read that report and got an idea. He hadn't had much success with his previous concoctions, such as his Globe of Flower Cough Syrup, but he got hold of some dried cola nuts, ground them up, stewed and strained them, added sugar, and mixed that into a tea with the addition of dried coca leaves, which were just coming into this country from South America. Pemberton advertised his drink as "an esteemed brain tonic and intellectual beverage," which everybody knew was just a fancy way of saying it was a hangover cure. He then added carbonated water and sold it over the fountain of his drug store, St. Jacob's Pharmacy. It went on sale as Coca-Cola on May 8, 1886. It was a modest success, but Pemberton had spent more in advertising and production than he made, and the next year he was forced to sell two-thirds of his sole ownership for $1,200.

Four years later still another Atlanta pharmacist, Asa Candler, bought Coca-Cola outright for $2,300, and by changing its emphasis from a nerve and brain tonic built it up into the popular drink it was to become over the next few years. He sold the syrup to druggists all over the country, and within five years it was available in every state in the Union. The reason it flew, back then, was because of the coca leaf, which, of course, contained cocaine. The cola nut had the caffeine, but it was the cocaine that made everybody feel so terrific.

Coca-Cola did so well over the counters that Candler was persuaded to bottle the beverage under contract, and the first bottling plant opened in Chattanooga, Tennesseee, in 1899. Business boomed, but in 1912 the U.S. government came along and made Coca-Cola decoke it's drink—they still used the coca leaf as the basis for their tea, but the cocaine was gone. By that time, though, cola had far surpassed root beer, sarsaparilla, and the rest to become the nation's leading soft drink, and Coca-Cola was by far the leader, outstripping all competitors and lucrative enough to allow Candler to sell out to Ernest Woodruff in 1919 for $25 million.

One of the reasons for Coca-Cola's dominance of the field was that at the time it was a better drink than its hundreds of cola competitors. But the other reason was that the company kept a battery of lawyers busy in courts around the country successfully suing any other brand that dared to use the word "cola." Early in the century they had staked a claim on the word, and within thirty years Coca-Cola had a mountain of court decisions in their favor to back up that claim.

By the time I got involved with Pepsi-Cola it already looked as if it might become a threat to Coca-Cola, so naturally a suit was instituted. Coca-Cola again claimed that we had no right to use the word "cola" in connection with any drink, and they got the biggest law firm in the United States to take us into the New York State Supreme Court in an attempt to shut us down. It was a very dangerous suit for us, because if Pepsi lost, we were out of business. I hired Dave Podell, one of the best trial lawyers in the business, to represent us, but the case against us looked pretty bleak. Coca-Cola had won lawsuits in every state where anybody tried to put out a drink with the name "cola" on it—something like 240 cases—and their lawyers appeared with volumes of decisions all bound in brown leather. It made quite a showing in court; quite a depressing showing for us.

I would go into the Pepsi offices in Queens at about eight in the morning and stay there until about nine-thirty, when I would go down to the courthouse to watch the proceedings. Every morning a big Coca-Cola truck would pull up in front of the courthouse and all these Coca-Cola men in livery would march in carrying volumes of books showing all the court cases they had won. It seemed overwhelming. The case they had won nearest to the New York area involved a company called Cleo Cola which once had a factory in

Orange, New Jersey. There they had won a unanimous decision, and Cleo Cola had gone out of business.

One night the evening paper carried an article on its financial page covering the case, and it mentioned that Coca-Cola had brought out the Cleo Cola decision as evidence against us. That's about all it said, but the next morning about nine, my secretary came in and said that somebody who sounded like a little old lady was on the telephone. She had seen the article in the paper the night before and would like to offer her condolences. Well, I'm always ready to talk to anybody, and I felt like condolences that morning, so I took her call. "Mr. Mack," said the tiny little voice, "my name is Mrs. Herman Smith. My husband was president of Cleo Cola, and Coca-Cola is going to put you out of business just like they did my husband. There isn't anything you can do about it, except make the best of it you can."

"Mrs. Smith," I said, "thank you very much. I'm afraid you're right. Our position is that 'cola' is a generic term referring to the nut, and that it doesn't belong to anybody, while they claim that they own the term, and it looks like the courts have backed them up so far. I don't believe their claim, and I honestly think we're in the right, but I don't know what's going to happen."

"My husband thought he was right too," she said, "but they still put him out of business. And I still have a photograph of the check they gave him. It was for $35,000. We cashed the check, of course, since it was the greatest amount of money my husband had ever seen, but I still have the picture of it on my wall. I look at it now and then to remind me of my late husband."

I could hardly believe what I was hearing. My mind was racing. "Mrs. Smith," I said, trying to control my eagerness, "may I send someone over to borrow the picture of that check. I'll take good care of it and of course I'll return it to you."

She agreed, and I sent a young man over to Orange to pick it up. We immediately rushed it down to the courthouse, and our lawyers were naturally very excited because there was nothing in the record of the court proceedings that mentioned any transfer of money. What Coca-Cola had done, in effect, was to buy the decision, and they had perpetrated a fraud in court by not disclosing it. When court opened, Dave Podell asked if Coca-Cola would mind returning to the case of the preceding day, the Cleo Cola decision, and Coca-Cola was delighted to do so. Dave walked to the bench and submitted the photograph of the check and marked it as our exhibit. He then turned to the lawyers for Coca-Cola and asked why their company had paid Mr. Smith $35,000 to agree to a decision.

There was great consternation in the courtroom, and the Coca-Cola people asked if they could look at the check. On the back of the check, below the endorsement, it said "Account H-13," and since the head of Coca-Cola's legal department in Atlanta was named Hirsch, it seemed to us that the "H-13" account might have been the legal department's private ledger, and that instead of winning all those hundreds of cases across the country, a lot of them had probably been bought off. Dave asked the court to requisition the H-13 ledgers from Atlanta, and the Coca-Cola lawyers, by this time all astir, asked for a three-day adjournment so that they could go to Atlanta and get them.

Early the next morning I got a long distance call from Robert Woodruff, president of Coca-Cola. He said he was coming up from Atlanta the next day and asked if I would join him for lunch at his apartment in the Waldorf Towers. I agreed, and after a couple of very, very dry martinis and some amiable chitchat he said: "You know, Walter, I've been thinking. This lawsuit between us isn't doing anybody any good, and it's just opening up a lot of channels for other colas and more competition. Don't you think we ought to settle it?"

I knew then that I had won. He didn't want to open a can of worms, because Coca-Cola may have bought a lot of their decisions—nobody knows how many for sure, maybe between 10 and 80 percent—and had apparently perpetrated a fraud by failing to disclose that these cases had not been decided "on the merits." I had him where I wanted him, so I took out a plain piece of Waldorf stationery that was on the desk and in ink across the top I wrote, "I, Robert Woodruff, executive officer and president of Coca-Cola Company, hereby agree to recognize Pepsi-Cola's trademark in the United States and will never attack it." I handed him the paper, he signed it, and that's how the Coca-Cola lawsuit was settled. It took Coke and Pepsi's lawyers three months and an inch-thick volume of papers to say the same thing. It was once again a stroke of luck on my part—blind luck, and Mrs. Herman Smith of Orange, New Jersey.

13

Up to this time I'd been dividing myself more or less equally between Phoenix and Pepsi, which was still a subsidiary of Loft, but my interest was leaning more and more toward Pepsi as an independent, full-time involvement. One of the first companies we divested ourselves of at Phoenix was United Cigar–Whelan Drug. I felt we had reached the point where there wasn't anything more we could do to help them, so I got my people together and said: "Look, we've got a drugstore at the corner of 59th and Madison Avenue, and across the street on the opposite corner is a Liggett Drug Store. My wife is on the other side of the street next to Liggett's. We're both selling the same type of merchandise and we've both got the same type of store. So tell me, why should my wife cross the street to go to Whelan's instead of Liggett's?"

One of my people thought we were a little cleaner, and I said, "Nonsense." Another thought we gave a little better service, and I said, "Forget it." They simply couldn't tell me why she should cross the street, and I knew it was time to leave. Whelan's didn't have any growth potential because it didn't serve a basic marketing function, and it was in good enough shape to sell, so that's exactly what we did.

Getting rid of Loft came next. The candy business itself is a lousy one (80 percent of its tonnage volume is in nickel and dime bars, and that didn't appeal to me very much), but once involved with Pepsi I became excited about *its* potential. So we sold off Loft and I moved over to Pepsi full-time. It was a case of the subsidiary becoming more attractive for potential growth than the parent, but it was almost impossible for me to run Phoenix and still find the time to reorganize and run Pepsi. So the decision was made to liquidate Phoenix, whose stock was already selling at high prices. The board of directors of Phoenix voted to distribute to each stockholder a proportionate amount of stock in the companies we owned; thus, a stockholder who owned 2 percent of Phoenix shares received 2 percent of the Pepsi shares that Phoenix owned.

Once Phoenix was no longer, I moved my base of operations from the relative comfort of 48 Wall Street to the Pepsi plant in Long Island City. The first order of the day, as far as I could see, was to set up a bottling franchise system for Pepsi-Cola. Coca-Cola had started their system in the days when trucks were drawn by horses, and had franchised areas only big enough to cover the distance a horse-drawn truck could go in a day to deliver Coca-Cola and bring back the empties to be reused. As a result, they had divided the United States into 1,150 franchise areas. When I came along in 1938–39, I divided the country into much larger areas, equivalent to the distance a motor truck could go in a day for delivery and return, so I franchised 550 areas.

In my travels around the country I found that there was always a wealthy bottler in each area, and that was the Coca-Cola bottler, while there were a lot of little bottlers who weren't making any money at all. So I went out and found the best of the little bottlers and tried to seduce them into taking Pepsi-Cola. A lot of them didn't want to challenge Coke, but to others Pepsi looked like a fine proposition. Many, however, didn't have the money to get started, so, using a little ingenuity, I gave them permission to use secondhand beer bottles. The beer boys used a twelve-ounce bottle, and there was an enormous flood of them all over the country at the time because it was too expensive to ship them all the way back to the home breweries to be refilled; they simply used new bottles every time. So I went to three of the largest secondhand-glass dealers in the country, bought up their entire stock, and let the franchise bottlers have them for a quarter of a cent a bottle. We then added a nice paper label with the trademark, our name and a crown, and shipped them out to the stores. Since some of the recycled beer bottles were green while others were white or brown, we had the damndest-looking collection of bottles you'd ever hope to see, but they all had a 2¢ deposit on them, which bottlers got in cash from the stores on delivery. Since they had paid only a quarter of a cent for each bottle, this gave them an extra 1¾¢ in working capital on each bottle. That quick infusion of cash was the only way I was able to finance my original bottlers with seed money.

They used up all the bottles I had bought in two years, but by then they had some fat on their bones and I got J. Gordon Carr, the man who designed the interior of Tiffany's, to design us an elegant new bottle with a baked-in label. This bottle cost 4¢, but it was classy, distinctive, and it too held twelve ounces. People had bought Pepsi in those funny bottles because it was a time when everybody was watching their pennies and Pepsi gave them twice as much for the same price as a bottle of Coca-Cola, so I didn't see any reason for changing what was one of our most important sales strengths.

I had very little money to invest in advertising at first, so I tried to spend as little as possible and make it go a long way. One of the first things I went into in 1939 was skywriting. A fellow named Sid Pike had an exclusive patent on a little plane that would spell things out with smoke. I made a deal with him that if he could keep the Pepsi name up in the air and legible for three minutes I'd pay him $50; if it didn't stay he wouldn't get a thing. Sid started out in Florida, spent about three weeks there, and then moved with the sun to other densely populated areas, spending from two to three weeks in each before going on. Some days it was windy up there and Sid didn't make much money, but most of the time there it was, all over the country, up in the air, the words "Pepsi-Cola." I had an exclusive at first with skywriting, and it made a huge impression. Not only had most people never seen skywriting before, but most had never heard of Pepsi-Cola. They made a beautiful team, and the skywriting helped make our product a household word.

My greatest stroke of luck, though, came at about the same time, 1939. One day my secretary came in to tell me that there were a couple of odd-looking fellows outside wearing white shoes, open shirts, and no coats, and they said they wanted to see me about some advertising matter. So in they came, and one of them, Bradley Kent, said. "Mr. Mack, we think we've got something here that might just fit in with your advertising." And the other fellow, Austen Herbert Croom, took out one of those old Victrolas that winds up on a spring and put on a phonograph record, and I heard for the first time:

> Pepsi-Cola hits the spot,
> Twelve full ounces, that's a lot,
> Twice as much for a nickel, too,
> Pepsi-Cola is the drink for you.

It was sung to the tune of the old English hunting song "John Peel," and it was music to my ears.

These were the days of radio, and everybody was tuning in to the same programs, but I found that when it came time for the commercials, everybody got up and went to the bathroom or started talking and nobody listened. I had already dismissed radio advertising as a waste of time, but here was something different. It was amusing, entertaining, and catchy—although at the time I had no idea just *how* catchy—and it was short, just thirty seconds. Best of all, it was different, and it caught my fancy.

"Tell you what I'll do," I said. "I'll give you $500 for it and I'll test it out. If it does for me what I hope it will, I'll give you another $1,500. If it doesn't work, I'll give it back to you so you can try it on somebody else."

They were delighted with the deal, so I took it over to NBC and asked if they would put it on and test it for me, but they refused, saying they never sold advertising air time in less than five-minute blocks. Then I went over to a classmate of mine from Harvard, Alan Marsh, who was a vice-president at CBS, and asked him if he would sell me thirty-second and sixty-second spots, and he told me I was crazy; nobody would sell me anything less than five minutes. As it turned out he was right; nobody at any of the big networks would consider anything less than five minutes, and this spot played only in a thirty- or sixty-second version. Even my own advertising agency argued against it, maintaining that the public wouldn't pay any attention to a little ditty unsupported by hard sell. They kept telling me that since I was just starting out I needed to tell *all* of my product's advantages *all* the time, and that this jingle was just a waste of that time.

Still, against all the odds, I knew I had something, so I went out to some of the little radio stations in New Jersey that weren't making much money; I was able to buy my thirty- and sixty-second spots from them, and they were the first to put the jingle on the air. When, after two weeks, the sales reports started coming back from those areas, there was no doubt that the thing had taken off, so I bought time on more and more stations and the jingle started getting talked about all over the country.

One day not too long after, Alan Marsh from CBS called me up and said, "Walter, damn your soul, the networks can't afford to have something a big success that didn't come through them, so we'll sell you your one-minute spots." NBC came on board soon after that. It's surprising what you can get into a thirty-second spot, but up until that time nobody had thought of it; that was the first commercial jingle ever heard on the air. Today, when I listen to some of the jingles that come pouring forth, I'm not so sure that I started such a good thing.

By 1941, that little jingle had been broadcast 296,426 times over 469 stations. In 1942 we had it orchestrated and distributed a hundred thousand copies of a full-length recording of it. And over the years it has been played as a march, a waltz, and a rumba, among other things. The jingle has gone into the annals of advertising history by now, along with the nickel bottle, but it did more to gain recognition for Pepsi-Cola than if we'd spent millions on billboard and print advertising, or on buying those five-minute radio spots that I was assured were the only way to advertise. It's a lucky thing I was in the office that day when those two odd-looking fellows with the white shoes dropped in for a visit. They, by the way, did all right out of it too, since they went on to become the jingle kings of their day and made a fortune.

That jingle really got Pepsi rolling, but Coca-Cola did everything in the world they could to stop us.

They couldn't take us to court anymore, but there were other tactics. Soon after I instituted my secondhand beer bottle scheme I got a call from Bob Woodruff asking if I could come down and have lunch with him in Wilmington, Delaware, where he was living at the time. So I went down and had lunch with him and he started pouring out those dry martinis. I don't know how many we had—it was more than I'd ever had before lunch in my life—but I made up my mind that I wouldn't have one unless he was having one too. If I was going to get drunk, he was going to get just as drunk, so by the time we sat down to lunch it was about three-thirty and we'd polished off about ten of them, and we were both just about holding our own. He didn't get down to business until after lunch, when he said, "You know, you're a newcomer to the soft drink business, so it can't mean that much to you, can it?"

I answered that it meant that I had a challenging and interesting job in an interesting field. "Well," he said, "I think I've got something more interesting for you. I own White Motors, and we need a president, and you're just the type of guy I want. You're making about $50,000 a year at Pepsi (which was true), and White Motors will pay you $250,000. And you can write your own ticket as far as a pension plan is concerned, with as long a contract as you want."

"Thank you very much, Bob," I said, "but I've just started this job and I can't walk out on it now. Money doesn't mean that much to me, but doing the job means a lot." We left it at that. The people at Coca-Cola, however, didn't leave it at that and went after us every which way. For instance, they would start rumors that our product was no good and that it was filled with chemicals, which, of course, was completely untrue; but worse than that, they physically got very rough. One of their tactics was to follow our deliveries into one of the big chain grocery stores like A & P. After we had set up our supply of Pepsi in cases and displays, the Coca-Cola truck would arrive, they'd pull our signs down, and they'd stack their cases right around ours so that the customers couldn't even see Pepsi. The Coke franchise in New York was run by a fellow named Jim Murray, and one day I went into one of the stores and watched what they were doing. The next day, I dressed a couple of our boys in A & P uniforms and stationed them in the A & P with cameras. When the Coca-Cola boys came in to do their stuff, we took pictures of them in action and I gathered the evidence together and went down to Mr. Murray's office and told him that unless it stopped immediately he was going to be faced with a lawsuit for tampering with other people's property. Needless to say, that particular harassment tactic was dropped immediately, but Coca-Cola had a bundle of other tricks up their sleeves, which they would pull out regularly over the next few years.

14

Although I remained active in politics all through this time, it seemed to me that I was much better at organizing and fund raising than I was at politicking, so after my defeat in 1932, I never ran for office again. I stayed pretty much in the background, but even then it was on the local level, working with the LaGuardia administration in New York City. I stayed out of the 1936 presidential elections because I felt that Roosevelt was a splendid man who had saved our country from revolution, but by the time 1940 rolled around, people seemed to be looking for a change, and it seemed like we Republicans might have a good shot at the White House.

In the meantime, Tom Dewey had become governor of New York, still riding the crest of his reputation as a fearless, crime-busting district attorney, and he wanted to be nominated for President in the worst way. I still had my own opinion of him from the early days, and it hadn't changed in the least. I knew he was a selfish, ruthless guy who would put his own grandmother on the block if he thought it might help him become President of the United States, and there was no way I could accept him as our candidate. Dewey thought he had the 1940 convention all wrapped up, but I was determined that this not be so.

In those days the conventions voted as a unit, with a state's delegate chairman announcing the candidate for whom that state would cast its entire block of votes. But at the 1940 convention, where I was a delegate from New York, I got busy and went to various other delegations and found that there were a lot of individuals who, like me, were not satisfied with Dewey. They thought that Wendell Willkie would make a fine President, but they were afraid to buck their states' political leaders. It was always "Alabama casts its twenty-one votes for Thomas E. Dewey," or whatever. Finally I got a bunch of them to agree that if I spoke up as an individual delegate from New York and raised a little hell, they'd back me up and maybe we could start a stampede.

During the third ballot it looked like Dewey was going to make it, and when they got down to New York, our chairman stood up and said, "New York casts its eighty-nine votes for Thomas E. Dewey," but I jumped up and demanded a recount. Well, all hell *did* break loose, as you can imagine, because this was

Dewey's home state. The gallery booed me, of course, and it took a long time for some sort of order to be restored, but they polled us individually—it was perfectly legal, but nobody had ever requested an individual recount of the delegates before—and in that go-around Willkie picked up fourteen votes from the New York delegation and the stampede was on. Other states began demanding recounts and individual polling, and on the sixth ballot we nominated Wendell Willkie. Dewey was in his hotel listening to all this on the radio, and he was ready to shoot me on the spot, but he had it coming to him, and I'm happy to say that he blamed me personally for keeping him from the Republican nomination in 1940.

It's always dangerous to say that things might have been different when we look at them with the clarity of hindsight, but I think the world might have been a very different place if Willkie had won that election. He was a brilliant lawyer, one of the best on Wall Street; a liberal; and an internationalist. He had written a book, *One World,* that was based on the principal that all our problems could be worked out if the great powers got together and helped one another. He wasn't a pacifist, but he wanted peace throughout the world and argued that it was possible if people worked together. However, he had never been in politics before, and instead of winning the election hands down, as he might have, he defeated himself.

When Willkie was nominated he was wonderful, his ideas were sound, and his vision broad, and I got to know him pretty well during the campaign. We had breakfast every third day or so and talked strategy, and he couldn't have been nicer, but about halfway through the campaign he changed completely. It all went to his head and he began to believe he was some sort of messiah. During the first part of his campaign he discovered that people looked upon him as a sort of hero, and he began to believe he was as great as they all were telling him he was. Now, that's the worst thing that can happen to anybody, and especially to a candidate for office, but Willkie began to believe his own press, and after that we couldn't even talk to him. I remember that several of us who were trying to organize his campaign went to him and said that there was a big rally going on in Texas and he ought to go down and make a speech, but he declined, saying that if the people of this country wanted him to lead them they would elect him, but he wasn't going down to Texas to seek their help. In effect, he was no longer running for elected office but was instead turning into the messiah he thought he was. Roosevelt won his unprecedented third term with 54 percent of the popular vote and 499 electoral votes, but I still contend that he didn't so much defeat Willkie as Willkie defeated himself.

After the election Willkie returned to his senses and to his law practice, where, soon after, his brilliance was to come to the aid of Pepsi-Cola. War had broken out all over Europe in August 1939, and although we would maintain our official neutrality until December 1941, the United States was gearing up for an involvement that was beginning to look more and more inevitable. In the meantime, international travel was drastically curtailed and entry into Europe literally impossible, so Coca-Cola chose 1940–41 as the time to sue Pepsi-Cola in the English Privy Council for infringement of copyright for using the word "cola." Woodruff's written agreement with me was limited to this country, and although Pepsi was not being produced or sold abroad at that time, if Coke had won in the Privy Council we at Pepsi would never have been able to go anywhere. Coca-Cola had been exporting to Britain since 1909, and for thirty years they had been exclusive in that market. Now it looked like we were growing fast, and they wanted to ensure their exclusivity. They really did think they owned the world. Since Coca-Cola was already established in Britain, they had a battery of lawyers already on the spot to argue the case before the Privy Council, while we, still a relatively small outfit, of course had nobody. And, because of the war, there was no way to get anybody over there. They thought they had us licked.

I went to see Wendell Willkie at his Wall Street office and asked if he would fly over to Britain and get together a team of lawyers to present our side of the case before the Privy Council. "Walter," he said, looking at me a little strangely, "there *is* a war going on, you know. How am I supposed to get over there?" I told him I was sure that if he went down to Washington and asked Roosevelt if there wasn't something he could do to help him, he would. Although they had run against one another, Willkie and Roosevelt were good friends, and the President had often asked Willkie's law firm to take on legal assignments for his administration. Willkie finally agreed to do it, but only if it would in some way benefit the war effort. I agreed, gave him a $25,000 retainer, and he went down to Washington to see his friend Roosevelt. The President said he would fly Willkie over on a transport plane if he would agree to go through London, which was then in the midst of the blitz, and make speeches on the President's behalf saying that America was with them and would see them through the war. Willkie jumped at the chance and flew over in a transport two days before our case was due to come to trial. He appeared before the Privy Council and they handed down a unanimous decision in favor of Pepsi-Cola. Then he went out and blitzed London on his own with speeches that did a great deal to make the British understand that they were not standing alone.

Willkie's trip was a great success on both counts, and for Pepsi it marked the end of our court cases with Coca-Cola over copyright. We agreed that after that we would refrain from battling before judges and would limit ourselves to fighting it out in the marketplace, but even in that open warfare Coca-Cola had the enormous advantage of size and political influence. They lost that last round in court, but soon after, they tried to hit us where it hurt by limiting one of our major raw materials, sugar.

Sugar is enormously important in soft drinks, and we continually had to guard against fluctuating prices. Back in 1939 I foresaw a big increase in world sugar prices and bought Pepsi an enormous sugar plantation in Cuba, some 40,000 acres, just to be sure we would have enough. Although I knew I wouldn't be able to import the sugar into the United States, at least I would be able to sell it in the world market at the increased price and thus offset the price hikes within the U.S. I went down to study the plantation and found that it was really very good. Sugarcane grows beautifully without fertilizer in Cuba because the topsoil is twenty-four feet thick. However, not only was it a natural for the area, but at the time, unfortunately, it was the only product they produced, and it kept the workers in a permanent state of poverty. The *colonas*, as the local Cuban peasants called themselves, lived in little thatched huts on the plantation. They worked like hell for four months cutting sugarcane by hand, and the other eight months they didn't have a thing to do, so they borrowed from the company store in order to live. Of course, they went into debt for eight months, paid it off in the four they worked, and then they were right back where they started. They never had a chance to get ahead, but at the same time they couldn't have been nicer people, and I wanted to help them in some way.

I asked why they didn't get some chickens and livestock, cattle and pigs, so that they could raise them during the eight months when they were idle and sell them in the markets in Havana (at the time, food was terribly expensive in Havana because it all came from Mexico or the United States), and the answer was that they didn't have any water except salt water, and you can't raise a chicken on that. I didn't believe that there wasn't fresh water somewhere, so I went back to the States and sent representatives from one of the biggest engineering firms down to the plantation to do some digging. They had to go down 4,000 feet, but up came pure, sweet water. I had them drill four wells and set about creating a community farm. I sent down cattle, chickens, feed, and seed, and they went to work, and in no time at all we had a terrific community operation going.

About two months later, George Walker, who was

running the sugar plantation and the project for Pepsi, called and told me to get down there fast. There was trouble brewing. That's all I could get out of him at the time, so I flew right down and there was an assistant secretary of the Cuban treasury to greet me. He said that he'd been there for a couple of days looking over our books and found that we owed the government $9 million in back taxes. I was astounded, since we paid our tax bill regularly. His answer was that perhaps we had been billed incorrectly, but the money was still owed. This went on for a bit, and finally he suggested that we go to lunch—alone.

We'd hardly sat down when he said, "Mr. Mack, you are ruining the economy of Cuba with your little project."

"Nonsense," I replied. "This will *make* the economy of Cuba. Can't you see how it is helping the people, your people."

"Exactly, and that is how you are ruining the country's economy. These men will never go out and cut cane for four months if they know that they can make a living another way. Cutting sugarcane is not pleasant, but it is the basis of our entire economy. If the *colonas* become independent of the plantation's company stores, there will be no reason for them to break their backs in *your* sugarcane fields."

The irony of it all was not lost on me. They were "my" sugarcane fields, but it was "his" country. The word of my experiment had spread all over Cuba, and all the *colonas* wanted to set up similar projects, but the government would not allow it. They agreed to forget Pepsi's newly found $9 million in back taxes if I agreed to seal off my wells and close down my farm; if

I didn't, they were sure that there were even greater back taxes to be found on closer examination of our books.

I could have hit that little bastard right then and there, but what good would it have done? I didn't want to let down the *colonas* now that I had given them a chance to make some money and some hope for their future and for their children's future, but on the other hand I couldn't let my company pay out millions in extortion taxes. So I did the only thing I could: I sold the plantation to three Cubans who just happened to be powerful senators. I never went back to check, so I can't be certain, but I heard that the wells were closed, the community project abandoned, and the plantation returned to its one-crop basis.

Batista was Cuba's dictator at the time. He took over in 1933, and even though they kicked him out the year after I left, 1940, he regained power in 1952 and milked his people for seven more years until Castro finally ran him out. If I had been a Cuban I'm sure I would have embraced Castro, because under the heel of the tyrants who ran the island as their own private company, the vast majority of people were frozen in the structure. There was no way they could move upward, and, of course, they were already down as far as they could go. A further irony to that story is that in an effort to protect its profits, a strong capitalist company by the name of Pepsi-Cola had gone into Cuba and set up Cuba's first communist commune simply as a logical step in order to improve the plight of its workers. If the Cuban government had followed our example elsewhere and grown with us, perhaps there would have been no need of the revolution twenty years later, but their blindness caused their own destruction. Cuba is certainly not the only example of this self-destructive policy of government—I've seen a lot of it over the past sixty years throughout the world—but in Cuba I dealt with it firsthand, and it made me feel powerless and sick at heart.

What the loss of our Cuban sugar plantation meant to Pepsi on a more immediate level was that we no longer had a safeguard when a quota was put on sugar and rationing went into effect in 1942. The law used 1941 as its base year and limited the amount of sugar any company could use to 80 percent of that year's consumption. For a company just getting started, 80 percent of the previous year is nothing at all; but for a giant, 80 percent still leaves them on top. We were still small potatoes in 1941, while Coca-Cola was already a giant, so it seemed that the sugar rationing would put a lot of my little bottlers out of business, and while I didn't want to seem unpatriotic, it also all looked a little fishy. The country was short on sugar, but not that short, and the man who was in charge of instituting the sugar rationing was Ed Forio, who just happened to have been a vice-president of Coca-Cola before resigning to take the government appointment.

Studying the world sugar situation, I saw that there was only one place you could get sugar that didn't have to come in by boat and so wasn't endangered by German submarines, and that was Mexico; so I put on my hat and flew down to Mexico City. I went to the head of the sugar cooperative there and told him I wanted to buy his entire surplus crop of sugar and I wanted to pay him 1½¢ over the going price. We drew up a five-year contract in which I agreed to buy a minimum of

40,000 tons a year. The only problem was that Mexico had a law which forbade the export of sugar. The only way around that was to build a plant in Mexico for the manufacture of Pepsi-Cola syrup and to ship that across the border to the distributors. Thus I would be abiding by Mexican law, which required that all sugar be consumed domestically, and by the U.S. law that forbade the import of sugar from a foreign country.

I built my plant in Monterrey, just across the border, put my syrup in barrels, and sent it across the border by rail for direct shipment to my bottlers. Soon after that, sugar rationing was reduced from 80 to 60 percent of the 1941 level, and that would really have forced my bottlers out of business, so my Mexican operation saved all our necks. Without it we would have gone under.

But none of it was all that easy. I had to fight all the way to bring Pepsi's syrup in from Mexico. Coca-Cola was a very wealthy company and had an inordinate amount of political influence, which I felt they were exercising unduly. So, the next thing I did was to go down to see Charles Wilson, the man who had been put in charge of all war production. I sat down in his office and said: "Charlie, you've got a phony running the rationing of sugar. He comes from my competition, Coca-Cola, and it's not fair, it's not right. Now unless he's gone within a week, I'm going to let the people of the United States know what you're doing down here, which is playing favorites. If you're doing it with him, I'm sure you're doing a great many other things, so you'd better get rid of him within the week or there's going to be hell to pay."

"Now Walter, calm down," said Wilson. "You know

we have to ration sugar, and Forio is doing the best job he can."

"Forget it!" I said, and stormed out, but three days later Ed Forio resigned and went back to Coca-Cola.

Soon after that, however, I got word from the war production board that Coke had lodged a complaint with them that we were bringing in sugar illegally from outside the country. I got a telephone call from Leon Henderson who was in charge of all rationing, asking me to come down to Washington. Once I got there he said that he understood that I was bringing in sugar illegally and that it had to stop. "Mr. Henderson," I said, "if you can prove I'm bringing in sugar illegally, then I will stop, but I'm not. I'm bringing in Pepsi-Cola syrup, and that's not sugar. There's nothing in the law as written to prevent candy from coming into the U.S., and there's nothing preventing honey from crossing the borders, so where is it written in the law that Pepsi-Cola syrup is illegal? Coca-Cola doesn't have a complete monopoly on the sugar business, you know, but I'll tell you what I'll do. Here's my contract with the Mexican government and the Mexican sugar exchange for not less than 40,000 tons a year. If the U.S. really is that short of sugar, I'll turn the contract over to you at cost and you can bring in the sugar yourself. But if you can't bring it in, there's no way you can stop me from bringing my syrup into this country and giving it to people indirectly."

Two days later Henderson called me up and said, "Mack, damn you, you know I can't get that sugar out of Mexico because of their law that won't allow the export of sugar unless it's part of a finished product."

"Well, Mr. Henderson, if you can't get Mexico to

change their law, you aren't going to be able to stop me, because if you do I'll put a full-page ad in every big newspaper in this country saying that I'm able to bring additional sugar into this country for consumption by the people of the United States and you can't so you're stopping me. It won't look very good for you, Mr. Henderson, so take your choice." He hung up, and that's the last I heard of it, but it saved my bottlers those lean sugar years.

15

The war years were especially good ones for Coca-Cola. That's when they made their big debut into Europe and the rest of the world, a debut made with the help of the U.S. government. The quartermaster general at the time was a man named George Summerfield, and he was a close friend of Jim Farley, who was not only big in the Democratic Party but just happened to be president of Coca-Cola Export. Farley made a deal with the government that wherever the troops went, they would have Coca-Cola, and since the only way they could be sure of getting it was to have a bottling plant nearby, Coca-Cola plants sprang up in Italy, France, Germany—everywhere—all built by Summerfield and the government. I raised holy hell about it because I wanted them to put up some Pepsi plants, too, but I never got a single one.

Of course, when the troops left, the plants were still there, and so was the acquired taste. The civilians in these places associated Coke with all things American, which at the end of the war was pretty good, so naturally once the troops left they kept up their affection for the drink. In the long run, though, it was good for Pepsi, because Coke was our advance man. When we finally went into Europe, Coke had already been there a couple of years and had prepared the way. We just went in under their umbrella and undersold them, so even though I didn't like it at the time, it didn't hurt us in the long run, and we came out of it pretty well overseas.

At home, though, Pepsi was doing well indeed. Our name was by then well established, and although we were still a baby when compared with the giant from Atlanta, Pepsi-Cola was a household word and hitting the spot all over America. Our three big canteens for service personnel were in Washington, San Francisco, and New York, and I know they did a lot for our boys passing through these big cities who might very well have felt a bit lost otherwise. Maybe Pepsi made them feel a bit more at home; at least we tried. The centers were equipped with good facilities—and of course free Pepsi—and one rather special treat: a chance for a free vocal recording shipped to wherever they might choose. It was better than a letter home, but like Hallmark and its greeting cards, we realized that not every soldier, sailor, or marine was at ease with words, so we offered them sixteen messages appropriate for Mom,

Dad, sweetheart, or whoever fit the bill. All they had to do was read the message into the microphone and we'd do the rest. One of my all-purpose favorites went something like, "Let me tell you, Uncle Sam is doing a good job keeping me in the pink of condition for you, honey, so don't be worrying about me." Today it looks a little corny, but we didn't worry about being corny during that war. National cynicism was still a generation away.

Pepsi was still selling in twelve-ounce bottles, as opposed to Coke's six-ounce bottles, and while our customers were getting twice as much for their money, my bottlers weren't, because the price of sugar, along with labor and transportation, had risen dramatically. By the end of the war we could no longer keep our price at a nickel, and rather than reduce the size of the bottle we simply had to up the price, first to six and finally to seven cents. We were hoping we had established ourselves so well that the public would go along, but we really were surprised when they did. At first we lost almost 20 percent of our volume, but within six months we were once more hitting our stride. The public realized that even with our price increase they were still getting a better deal than if they bought two nickel bottles of Coke, and I thought they were getting a much better drink. The jingle that had circled the world with "Twice as much for a nickel, too" had to go, but we retired it gracefully—it had certainly done its job well—and replaced it with "More bounce to the ounce," which had a nice ring to it, especially at the cash register.

During the time I was with Pepsi I remained active in politics, organizing behind the scenes, and one of the first things I did at Pepsi-Cola was to tell all our bottlers to get involved in local politics and to make sizable contributions to their state senators and members of congress. I was very aware of Coca-Cola's political wallop and wanted Pepsi to have a say in government too. There are a lot of things that are perfectly legitimate, but if you don't have influence in your local government, your state capital, or in Washington, you can't get them done. There's nothing I ever did with my Pepsi people that I wouldn't do in the open; there's nothing wrong with having friends in government—that's what our government is all about—but I always made sure that our contributions were clean. Payoffs are nothing more than cheap corruption, and that was never my style or way of doing business before, during, or since my years with Pepsi.

But influence in government is an entirely different matter. As a leading businessman, my services to government were always on a volunteer basis. During the war I helped organize fund-raising rallies in Madison Square Garden, and in the spring of 1945 I chaired the committee that planned the mammonth V-E Day celebrations in Central Park. I'm not patting myself on the back, because I saw it as my civic duty, but at the same time, these functions quite naturally helped me gain a certain amount of influence in certain important circles. But one place where I didn't have any clout, however, was with Robert Moses, New York's autocratic parks commissioner.

Moses was a thoroughly brilliant man who accomplished some extraordinary things, but he was extremely arrogant, and nobody could tell him what to do. During his forty-four-year reign he didn't let many people get in his way as he went about building highways, bridges, and parks, but he never did budge me. We had a big Pepsi plant on the East River right across from the United Nations, and on the roof I put a huge sign that flashed our name on and off.

One day Moses called me up and said: "Walter, I want you to take down that sign. It's right opposite the United Nations and it flashes on day and night."

Of course I already knew this, so I said: "Bob, that's just great. I love it that way. It gives them all something to think about, since we are a typically successful American business. We're good capitalists."

This didn't make him too happy, so he threatened to pass a law to make me take it down if I didn't do it voluntarily. My reaction was to tell him that was fine, go right ahead. So Moses introduced a measure in the City Council stating that there would be no signs within a certain radius of the U.N., and my plant came well within that radius. The next day the borough president of Queens, who was a friend of mine, called me up and asked me what I wanted him to do about it. I said, "Kill it or let it die in committee, because I'm going to keep my sign there, and if they try to make me take it down I'll tie them up in so many lawsuits it'll stay up there anyway." The bill never got out of committeee. It stayed there for four years, and Bob Moses never could understand why he couldn't get a law passed.

But he didn't give up, and one day he called me down to have lunch with him in his tower suite overlooking the Triborough Bridge, and after a while he said, "What can I do to get you to take that sign down?"

"Nothing," I said. "It stays."

"Okay, I'll make a deal with you. Will you allow me to put through a law that no new signs can be put up opposite the U.N.?" I said, "Of course," and told my friends to let it go though. No new signs have gone up since, but Pepsi still burns brightly.

Soon after that, Moses tried to get my building condemned so that he could build a park on the site, but when he found he couldn't get that bill through either he came to me and asked if I would simply sell him the property. "No," I said, "I won't sell it to you, but if you'll find me another suitable space on the river so I can bring in my sugar boats and still have a convenient way into the city I'll give it to you. Of course you'll have to buy the new place and pay for the move, but I don't want to stand in the way of your new park." About six months later he came to me and said that it would take about $17 million to move me over to New Jersey and he didn't have that much, so Pepsi is still across the river from the U.N., and I became one of Bob Moses's least favorite people.

Not only did I feel it was important that we as individuals become politically involved in the community, but I felt it was the duty of the company to institute a series of programs of a nonpolitical nature along the same lines. The most successful of these was the college scholarship fund, which we began right after the war. With the help of a number of prominent educators and college presidents across the country, we set up a series of national scholarships completely financed by Pepsi, but we weren't looking for scholars, we were looking for leaders, and that was the big distinction. There are a lot of men and women who have graduated from college with a great deal of book knowledge but who are not leaders. I decided that what I wanted to develop in the United States was leaders, so I set up my own rules for the scholarships. The basic rules were that the graduating class of every high school in the country vote for the five members they thought most likely to succeed; it had nothing to do with marks, only leadership. Then those five took examinations for scholarships. Basically it meant that those taking the exams were already potential leaders and the ones who had high enough scores to qualify for the scholarships also had knowledge. It was a terrific idea, and in eight years we sent over five hundred men and women to college. It cost Pepsi over a million dollars. By today's standards that's not much to pump back into the public coffers, but in the late forties it was quite a sum, so much so that soon after I left, the company discontinued the scholarship program, much to my disappointment. However, it had done such a good job that the idea was picked up and backed by others in private industry and grew into the National Merit Scholarship awards we have today.

When we first set up the program, each state was to choose two students for the scholarship, but I soon found out that the blacks could never win because their educational background was such that they didn't really have much of a chance of competing with the whites, especially in the segregated parts of the country, so I established separate scholarships for blacks in each state. In the end, every state had the right to choose four students, two whites and two blacks, since that was the only way I could get the blacks on scholarship. I knew it wasn't entirely fair or even proper, but I also knew it was the only way it could be done.

I had run into a similar situation earlier when I found that the unions at my big Pepsi plant in Long Island wouldn't allow black people on the production line. I had ten production lines at the time and they were all white, so I built two more lines and made them all black and forced the unions to take them. As a result, I was the first to get blacks into the soft drink and teamsters unions. Again, it might not appear fair, but it was a pragmatic step at the time, and it worked itself out.

In 1947 I instituted something else that apparently no one had ever thought about before: I opened up my stockholders' meetings to the stockholders. Now, it's true that stockholders are always invited to the annual meeting of any company, but there had never been any real effort to get them to come. I made that effort, and even went so far as to hold five big stockholders' parties, two in New York and one each in Los Angeles, Chicago, and Jacksonville, Florida. And they came. Out of the 25,000 or so Pepsi stockholders, over 8,000 showed up, and together we drank over 15,000 bottles of Pepsi and had a whale of a time. At first, people thought it was a bit of a joke—just another publicity stunt—and while it may have been terrific for publicity, it was more than just a stunt, and certainly no joke. Not only did I get to know a lot of new stockholders—and every one of them is important—but they got to know their company, and as a result we thereafter had 8,000 new Pepsi rooters and salesmen spread out across America, which is no small number for a growing company.

16

Once a year the top financial writers across the country gave a dinner at the Waldorf to which they invited all the nation's leaders in business, politics, medicine, science—all the top brass—and it invariably turned out to be a meeting of the most powerful people in the country. After one of these dinners, Jack Forest, who was then the senior financial editor for the *New York Times*, asked me to join a few of the others for cheesecake and beer, so at about one o'clock, a dozen or so of us went over to Lindy's. We were sitting around a big round table just generally going over the events of the evening—who was there, what was up, and so forth—and we all started to compare notes on the famous men who had been at the dinner. Somebody brought up the question of what all these men had in common. Some had worked their way up in their field, while others had either inherited big or built from a small inheritance. Some had been educated at the finest schools, while others were largely self-taught. Some were experts in one particular field, while others moved easily between industry, education, and government. Nobody fit into any category, but we finally figured out there was one common denominator shared by every leader in the country—and this could be applied throughout the world: They all had a terrific amount of energy. They didn't wear down in tough spots, and they didn't melt away. We all agreed that this was the only thing all of them had in common.

Nothing could be truer. Even today, I'm not tired after a full day, and I've always had a surplus of energy; but this same energy that I've relied on over the years to pursue my dual careers in business and politics has also managed to get me into all sorts of mischief. Ever since those first days with Aunt Nina, I was on some sort of prowl. If there had been a stabilizing influence in my life, perhaps this might not have been so, but my marriage to Marian was a sham, and there was no home at home, so I took my pleasures elsewhere, and my appetite was rather outsized.

And I was certainly not alone in my prowls. All the married women with whom I carried on during the twenties and thirties were upstanding, respectable ladies, yet they would go to the most extraordinary lengths to insure that we would spend the night together. They would do the damndest things, and sometimes I'd be scared to death, but it never seemed to bother them. I often wondered what their husbands were doing while I was playing with their wives.

One of the women I became friendly with was married to an enormously wealthy man. Her husband was a lawyer with millions, they had three attractive daughters, and she had everything in the world a person would want; yet she'd call me on the telephone at the office and make the most elaborate arrangements for a rendezvous. Once, for example, she called and said that she was going down to visit her daughter at Foxcroft, a girl's school just outside Washington. She was leaving Friday afternoon on the sleeper and had booked two adjoining staterooms. She told me my ticket was in an envelope in my name at the Harvard Club, if I'd care to join her for the trip. Naturally I *did* care to join her, and although I never got to see Foxcroft, it was one of the more pleasant train journeys I can remember. Other times she'd call and say her husband was working late so how about coming out to her place and she'd make a little picnic supper for us on the beach. This went on for quite a while, and although there was no danger to me, in her community and in her position she was exposing herself to an enormous risk. Still, she did it, and I don't think I was the only one; she knew too many tricks for a beginner.

One night I was out for dinner with friends when I ran into the daughter of one of the wealthiest, best-known families in Locust Valley. She was a beautiful, spirited girl, and I went over to join her table after dinner for a drink. We put quite a bit away and she leaned over and whispered in my ear the kind of invitation I always found hard to resist. She asked me what I was doing later on, and since it was already "later on" I told her that my next appointment was at Pepsi-Cola at nine in the morning, so she suggested that we drive out to her family's home and spend the night together. We got into her little runabout and drove out to Locust Valley, and as we got near her house she told me to get down in the rumble seat. So I got out of the car, she closed me in the trunk, and as we drove past the gate she saluted the guard at the entrance. She pulled up in front of the house and whispered to me to stay put for a few minutes while she went in to check to see if the coast was clear. She went in, brought the elevator down, and whisked me up to her room for the night. We got up at five-thirty, or rather we left the house at five-thirty, and she drove me to the station so that I could catch the six o'clock train to be at my desk by nine.

Neither of these two examples is an isolated case; my energy had to go somewhere, and I figured if these girls wanted to play, I was willing. None of it was serious, and at no time did I feel that I was cheating on my wife. What was there to cheat on—an empty, meaningless marriage? Marian and I grew further apart as the years went on, and after her four attempts to have children, I thought we could perhaps bridge our gap if we adopted; so we did, a boy and a girl, but it was a mistake. She didn't want to have any part of motherhood. I thought having the children might bring her around and make her more understanding of life, but she didn't like them and she didn't want the obligation of raising them, so basically Florence Ann and Tony were turned over to governesses. I did what I could, when I could, but I knew all along that it was no way to raise children.

While I was running Phoenix Securities a new secretary came in to work for me, Ruth Juergensen, and while she wasn't the best typist in the world, she was bright and personable and quite a looker, so I took her on. When I moved over to Pepsi, Ruth came over with me, and I put her in charge of Personnel to build up our organization. At the same time she remained my special assistant and did all my personal work, so she knew exactly what was going on all the time. Our relationship was strictly professional; although she was familiar with the details of my personal life, she was not a part of it. For instance, I was seeing one girl who was enormously wealthy and who always used the name "Mrs. Alexis Smith" when she called me. That wasn't her real name and Ruth knew it, so when she called up and said, "Would you tell Mr. Mack that Mrs. Alexis Smith is on the telephone," Ruth would come in and say "That phony is on the line again," and we'd have a good laugh over it. She was just my secretary, and I didn't have to account to her, but she knew all about my playing around and she knew all about the women—I was always suspicious that she listened in on some of our telephone calls, but what the hell—and over the years we developed a strong relationship, but still kept it on a professional level.

My mother became very fond of Ruth. By that time she was a widow, and when she went up to Lake Placid for the summer she would always ask Ruth up to spend a few weeks with her. My mother was a great woman, a true thoroughbred, and during the summer I would try to get up to the Adirondacks to visit her, and sometimes Ruth would also be there. Gradually I realized that I was falling in love with Ruth and decided that it was time to straighten out my private life, which was a mess no matter which way you looked at it.

The situation with Marian was getting absolutely impossible. She was completely irrational, and all the warnings I had earlier ignored about her insanity were coming true. She would sit down at the dinner table and suddenly scream, "I've had enough," and throw her plate across the room at the butler. And as bad as she treated the servants, she treated the children even worse. I knew the only thing to do was to face matters head-on, so one day I sat down and as calmly and rationally as I could said: "Marian, you know our marriage doesn't mean anything and it hasn't for many years. We haven't lived together since God knows when. You'd be better off on your own, and I'd be better off going my own way. I want a divorce." She was very calm and asked me if I was in love with somebody else. I answered that I might be, but that was not the only reason. She said she'd think about it, and left. I didn't want to hurt her feelings, and I wanted to leave her peacefully, but I felt she wasn't going to let that happen. And I was right.

I came home for dinner the following night and found that a very attractive girl, who had recently been divorced from a famous actor, was dining with us. The three of us had a pleasant supper and then Marian said she was tired and suggested that the two of us go out on the town and have some fun together. I knew there was something going on, so we went out to a club and I made up my mind to get this girl tight so I could find out what it was. We drank and drank and finally I said, "Okay, what is this all about."

The girl, by now quite drunk, said: "Your wife wants

me to be your mistress so that you won't get a divorce. I've agreed to give it a try, and I've got an apartment where we can spend the night."

"There's something more, isn't there?" I said.

"Yes," she answered. "Marian has agreed to pay me $25,000 a year to play your mistress."

I told her it was the craziest thing I'd ever heard and I certainly wasn't going to get involved in a deal like that. She was a great-looking gal and a nice one besides, but here was one I couldn't sleep with under any circumstances.

The next night I went home and told Marian it was all over and I intended to get a divorce. She carried on, said she wouldn't give me one, and suggested I simply set up this other woman I claimed I was in love with in some sort of living arrangement—anything I wanted, except what I really wanted: out. Marian downright refused to talk of divorce and said she would fight me all the way, so I walked out, got myself a good lawyer, and headed for Nevada to get my own divorce.

My lawyer sent me to a beautiful little ranch called the Tumbling DW which is in Carson City, just outside Reno. Most people were able to get their divorce in a couple of months—and there were about twelve or fifteen of us waiting out our time together—but because Marian refused to recognize the Nevada divorce as legal, I had to stay out there and open a branch office of Pepsi-Cola in Carson City. As soon as the divorce came through, Ruth came out and we were married in Carson City by the Chief Justice of the State of Nevada. Still, I couldn't go back to New York, because at that time the state did not recognize a Nevada divorce, and if I stepped across the border, Marian would have thrown me in jail for bigamy. The only solution was to set up Pepsi's operating offices in Newark, and all the executives had to come out by train to me. Ruth and I lived in Newark for about a year, in official sin, until finally my lawyers worked out a settlement with Marian whereby I paid her $50,000 a year alimony plus support for the children. She needed the money like she needed a hole in the head— it was just her way of getting revenge—and I figure that over the years I've paid her over $2 million, which is a hell of a lot when she didn't need it.

I recently came back from a promotional tour of the Midwest, and on one of the television talk shows the host asked me what person had most influenced my life over the years. Nobody had ever asked me that before, so I had to think a minute, and suddenly the answer became clear: Ruth. She changed my life and my habits overnight. She gave order to my life, a sense of purpose where none had been before, reason where there had been confusion. After Ruth came into my life I was able to channel my energies into business and politics and still have a home life, which was something that I'd never ever had before.

The first test actually came while I was still out in Nevada waiting for my divorce to come through. Ruth was in the East, and I was out there on the ranch surrounded by divorcees, all of whom wanted to sleep with somebody. The room next to mine was occupied by a beautiful woman who had been married to one of our most prominent bankers. She wanted to play around, but for the first time in my life I said no. I'm going to marry Ruth, I thought, and I'm going to be true to her. And overnight, that was that.

I had always enjoyed people and their companionship, and I'd always felt that you don't really know a person intimately until you have your head on the same pillow. I needed the warmth, the friendship, and the understanding that came with that. It did great things for me, gave me new energy and inspiration, and it helped me see a lot of life. I have no regrets about the first forty-eight years of my life, I've never had a bad experience, and if I had it to do over again I would probably do it exactly the same way. I never forgot the advice of that old sea captain and I never missed a real opportunity, but until I married Ruth I was going through the motions without any emotions. Up until 1943 I had been lucky enough to be in all the right places at all the right times. I'd enjoyed myself, learned a lot, knew a hell of a lot of wonderful people, and had been extremely lucky at every turn in business, but something was obviously missing. Ruth filled that void with love, and finally I realized what a truly lucky man I was.

In 1944 Ruth gave birth to our son, Walter, and two years after that to our daughter, Alice, while at the same time raising my two adopted children, Florence Ann and Tony, as her own. Florence Ann turned out beautifully, and for all practical purposes Ruth is her mother; she is our child. Tony didn't turn out quite so well. He was nothing but a problem from the beginning, and no matter what we tried to do we couldn't seem to break through to him. At school he was always fighting with the other boys and getting into difficul-

ties. I had to send him away to special schools for difficult children, but he never stayed anywhere for long.
He was always running away and I'd have to go search-
ing for him or get the state police out to find him. We
sent him to a number of child psychiatrists, but none
of them seemed to help.

He finally enlisted in the Navy, but he ran away
from boot camp in Chicago and was missing for more
than six months. The Navy went out looking for him,
and I hired a team of private detectives to try to
track him down; eventually we located him sleeping
on a bench in a railroad station in Albany, New York.
I sent him back to the psychiatrists, but they told me
to forget him and let him find his own level, which was
about all I could do.

I've always felt that I was as liberal in my personal
outlook as I was in my politics, and Tony's problems
were his own. It wasn't for me to try to force my
values on him, but I can't help regretting that he
turned away from me much as I turned away from my
father.

When my mother died she left a $50,000 trust fund
for each of my four children. The funds were left in my
name to administer and were to be turned over to the
children when they reached twenty-one. By the time
he reached that age, Tony was living in California, and
one day he called me and said he wanted me to send
him all his money right away. I told him I didn't want
him to take it all at once. I would have the income
from the trust sent to him regularly so that he could
live on it, but I wanted to continue administering and
investing it for him. This went on, back and forth, for
about three months, until one day his lawyer called

and said that according to the will Tony was entitled to all the money to do with whatever he wished, and he demanded that it be sent immediately. I called Tony and said the money was on its way but added that if I found out he had touched the principal, that would be that. "Tony, I'm going to tell you something. I'm sending you money to help you, to support you. You can get an income from that trust fund through investments, but if you use up the principal and squander it, forget about me. I won't send you any more, you'll be on your own."

Tony took that $50,000, hired a car, and went to Las Vegas with one of his friends. Within four months he was penniless, and soon after that he came to me. "No soap," I said. "Go to work." It was a tough thing to do, but it was the only way, and he eventually straightened himself out. He finally married a much older woman who had four children of her own, and they're all getting along together beautifully. I think they married one another for mutual security, possibly the security he felt, wrongly, that he never had with Ruth and me. I don't know, but he is happy at last, and that's what's important.

Because my own father was very strict, I never wanted my children to do things with me out of respect or out of fear; I wanted them to do things because we enjoyed doing them together. I wanted to be on the same wavelength. It never worked with Tony, and I never knew why until it was too late, but with the other three it paid off. I remember when Florence Ann, who was the eldest, would come back from parties and sit on my bed while we traded stories and the latest gossip. With Alice too I've always been able to talk quite frankly, as if we were the same age. Together with Tony, we were a very close-knit family. Every year we would all go away together for a month or so, someplace where we could really get away from it all and get to know each other all over again. One year we went out to a ranch in Wyoming, another time into the mountains out west, and still another time we toured Europe. Whenever we went, though, we would be together for a month. It was a time reserved for us as a family.

My good luck seems to have rubbed off on both my daughters, because they've managed to turn into fine women, and that's not always so easy these days unless you have luck on your side. But it is Walter who really inherited the dumb blind luck that has seen his old man through these past eighty-five years, and with Walter it saved his life. He was a captain in the Marine Corps stationed in Vietnam, and his company was way out in the boondocks guarding Highway Number One. They were living like animals out there, underground during the day, and when they came out at night, he told me later, he had a feeling when the enemy was around. It was just intuition, but when his hair stood on end, he knew they were there. One night when they came out, Walter just knew the enemy was around, so he kept his men back while he moved ahead with three others to clear out a forward area. He was standing in the road with his lieutenant assistant, the radio operator, and his field man, when they heard a bomb whistling overhead. They all dived for the ditch on the side of the road as the thing burst right near them, and of the four of them who hit that ditch, he was the only one who got up. Now if that isn't dumb luck, I don't know what is, but the good Lord seems to be looking after Walter just as he always has looked after me.

17

Basically, I'm the sort of fellow who likes to build things, and when I've gone as far as I can go and I'm stymied, it's no longer interesting or exciting. I've never really worked a day in my life, since the things I've done, the planning and the building, have all been fun, and that's not work. To me, business is a game of chess for high stakes with human pawns, and if it ceases to be that and becomes difficult, it's work, and it's not for me. There are plenty of people around who can handle the day-to-day running of a company better than I can; I'm a high-priced builder, not a desk-bound executive content to see his company coasting along, because I know that if you don't move ahead, you go backwards.

Competition is always moving ahead, and if you don't do things ahead of them, if you aren't creative before they are, then you're slipping behind.

I reached that stage with Pepsi-Cola in 1949. We were second in the United States and expanding in Europe, but we were doing the same humdrum thing that Coca-Cola was doing. We had reached the point where we were doing 20 percent of the cola business, and from there on out it was just routine plugging, which is something that I wasn't interested in doing. I wanted to revolutionize the soft drink business and bring it up to date. Nothing short of that would do.

When I took over Pepsi before the war I wasn't smart enough to realize that the grocery store revolution I was involved with during the early part of the Depression was just the beginning. I never thought that chain stores and supermarkets would completely replace the little Mom-and-Pop stores that were the backbone of America's retailing, and so when we set up Pepsi-Cola we did so along the already established lines of franchising bottlers and delivering directly to the store. That was the only way we could hit the thousands of little outlets that dominated the American scene at the time. But after the war all that changed. By then most other products were being delivered to a central warehouse which then delivered them to their own stores, such as A & P and Grand Union. It was only in the soft drink industry that we were stuck with the outmoded distribution system of delivering directly to the outlet.

The beer boys had been doing well by putting their product into cans and shipping it from the breweries to the retail warehouses, which in turn distributed it to the various stores. I couldn't see any way of expanding significantly unless we completely revolutionized along the same lines, so I got together with George O'Neil, one of my former vice-presidents from Pepsi who had retired with a franchise in Westchester County, and we built a canning plant in New Rochelle, New York. Continental Can made up some special cans for us— twelve-ounce versions sprayed with a vinyl coating so that the drink wouldn't pick up any metallic taste— which we used, and shipped our canned Pepsi directly to the local Westchester warehouse of A & P. Then we sat back and waited for our own little revolution to begin. We didn't have to wait long. Within two weeks my legal department was screaming "foul": "What are you trying to do, ruin the company? Here's a letter from the Pepsi bottler in New Haven. Here's another from the bottler in Hartford. And another from the bottler in Springfield. They're all saying that somebody is selling Pepsi-Cola in their exclusive area and if the company doesn't do something about it they're going to sue us for millions."

So I asked my lawyers, my bright boys, to figure out a way we could deliver to warehouses and not be forced to go to the front door of every store, and about a week later they came back with the answer: The only way to do it would be to buy up all the franchise bottlers. Now there wasn't enough money in the world to buy out those bottlers, because they were already making too much money, so I decided it might be time for me to go. But first I was going to try to put up a fight. If Pepsi's board of directors wasn't going to let me modernize by putting Pepsi into cans, eliminate the middleman, and do what everybody else in the grocery business was doing, I'd have to get my own board of directors.

The word got out that it looked like there was going to be a proxy fight between me and the board, and out of the clear sky the bottler from Detroit, a man by the name of Walter Dawson, came into my office and handed me a check for $50,000. "I want you to throw the bastards out," he said, "if that's what you want to do. Clear the whole board if you think it will help. I'm behind you all the way." Then along came another guy from out west who gave me a check for $75,000, and the money started coming in. Before I knew it I had $375,000 in the bank in my name to be used completely at my discretion to go into a proxy fight and clean house. Maybe then I would be able to do some of the innovative things I wanted to do, but even then it was only a maybe.

This reality was brought home to me when Joe Lapedes, who headed a big group of Southern bottlers, came in to see me. He sat down in my office and said: "Walter, I understand you've got a heavy war chest and you're ready to go into a big proxy fight, but is that what you actually want to do? You're going to set bottler against bottler, because once you start this, it won't stop. The very people that you've spent so many years building up, you're going to pull apart. You're going to hurt and maybe even destroy the whole organization that you've worked so hard to create. Why don't you compromise and step aside as president and chief executive officer and become chairman of the board instead. I'm sure we can get you a contract so that you can leave if it doesn't work out, but this is one battle you can't really win."

What he said made sense. I had gone about as far as I possibly could with Pepsi. I wouldn't be able to modernize, because I was stuck with the franchise system, and I knew that it would just lead to frustration, so I told them to go ahead and work out a contract for me as chairman of the board. I returned the entire $375,000 to the bottlers who had sent it to me, and I allowed myself to be kicked upstairs. They gave me a salary of $120,000 a year to do very little except stay out of the industry and stay out of their hair, but I only stayed around about a year and then I got out for good. I still had a lot of friends at Pepsi and remained a consultant so they could come to me for advice from time to time, but I never went back to company headquarters.

After I left, Pepsi's management started making a series of bad decisions and had a lot of labor trouble (there was never a single strike while I was running Pepsi), but I stayed clear of it. The strange thing about it, though, is that all the members of the board I had planned to replace started dying off soon after I left; within three years they were all dead. I can honestly say I had nothing to do with that.

While I was still president of Pepsi I hired a man named Alfred Steel and made him vice-president in charge of sales. He came from Coca-Cola and was a hell of a good salesman but a lousy financier, so naturally when I left they made him president. At the time he was married to an awfully attractive woman who originally came from Atlanta; she was as sweet as could be, but I guess Al figured she wasn't big enough to be the wife of the president, so he divorced her soon after and married Joan Crawford. I'd known Joan for some time because she'd been on the USO board with my wife Ruth during the war, and I always thought she was a

177

great gal, a tough, two-fisted drinker, and a hell of a lot of fun. Of course, I didn't know anything about her personal life—none of us did—and I'd never had any business dealings with her, but I did know she could give and take with the best of them.

Al wanted to impress her, so he bought a little island in Bermuda, right off Hamilton, and built this enormous stone house on it. It was to be his wedding gift to Joan, but being as careless with money as he was, he didn't get around to paying for it. Instead he charged the building of the house and all the furniture in it to Pepsi-Cola and ordered the treasurer to pay the bills. Still, he kept it in his name, and when the auditors came around during his second year as president they found that Al Steel owed the corporation $320,000. They insisted this discrepancy be reported to the stockholders at the next meeting, according to the law, and since I was still serving on a consultancy basis, the legal department came down to see me about it. They told me what a mess they were in and asked me what they should do about it. All I could say was: "Keep away from me with this one. I don't want anything to do with it. I'm no longer on the board, I'm just a consultant, so this is not my problem." And I'm certainly glad it wasn't.

The directors didn't want to fire Al, since he was doing a good job in spite of his way of handling money. So one of the bright lawyers came up with a bright idea. While disclosing the discrepancy at the annual meeting, they would also ask the stockholders to approve an option for Al to purchase 100,000 shares of Pepsi stock at $3.50 under the market value. He could then sell it at a profit of $325,000 to $350,000, pay the company off, and everybody would be in the clear. The annual stockholders' meeting was held on the morning of the first Wednesday in May, and it was nip and tuck right up to the wire whether the stockholders would approve the plan or not, but on the Tuesday before the meeting the secretary of the company called Al and said they had finally gathered enough proxies to approve his option the next day.

That night he and Joan went out to celebrate the fact that they would soon be out of hock, he'd be squared off with the company, Joan would be able to move into her big château down in Bermuda, and everything would be hunky-dory. They really went to town that night and came in at about two in the morning drunk as fools; and while they were waiting for the elevator to take them up to their apartment on East 55th Street, Al Steel dropped dead of a heart attack. So, of course, he never did get that stock option. Had he lived twelve more hours, he would have been cleared of debt, but instead he left his widow holding the bag for $320,000 and the threat of scandal.

Joan was a rich woman in her own right, because she had saved every penny she ever earned, but she wouldn't give up any of her money. She was a tough cookie who had worked hard for it, and she wasn't about to see it disappear because her husband of a very short time had been a fool over money and neglected to leave her anything but debts. At the same time, however, any indebtedness or hint of scandal was abhorrent to her, so she went to the board and made a deal. If they would give her the job of doing public relations, with a five-year contract at $65,000 a year, she would turn the salary back over to them and that way she'd pay off the debt. It seemed the only solution, so the board gave her the job and she went out and did a hell of a good one. She kept the house in Bermuda and more than paid off the debt. In the years after Steel's death she never appeared without a Pepsi or a Pepsi logo somewhere in the vicinity. I remember seeing a horror movie she made during that period, a terrible movie in which there's a scene where she brings some girl into the kitchen and there's a big Pepsi cooler right there on the kitchen table. And then Joan opens the refrigerator and it's filled with nothing but Pepsi. I think she must have had something in her contracts saying she wouldn't appear without Pepsi. If you wanted Joan Crawford, you had to take Pepsi.

Joan did such a good job that later on they made her a member of the board of directors, but she never really had any stock in the company and never any position besides that rather honorary one on the board. Of course, she gave the impression to everyone that she was chairman of the board—or at the very least Miss Pepsi-Cola—but then, that was all part of her act. Don Kendall, who was president disliked the attention Joan was receiving and tried to fire her a number of times because she was going around behaving like it was her company, but he never could get rid of her because of all the publicity attached.

As for all those stories about Joan going around spiking her Pepsi with vodka, they can be completely discounted. Joan was a great vodka drinker and she got drunk an awful lot, but she would never mix her Pepsi with vodka, because she never drank anything *but* vodka.

IV

The Recent Past,
the Present,
and, as Always, the Future

18

Once again I was lucky to leave Pepsi-Cola when I did. Looking back, I had a good time with them, but my time was up. I had built a good organization, an aggressive organization that had taken a nonexistent product and pushed it up to 20 percent of the market in a little more than a decade. In the thirty years since then they've managed to push that share up only another 5 percent, but now the organization is overmanned, everybody is out for everybody else's job, and every one of them is scared to death that they're going to be the next one fired. That's not the kind of organization I could ever be a part of, and so I was well out of it. I remained as a consultant to Pepsi until 1957, during which time, my contract said (in small print), I couldn't go into the soft drink cola business, but I certainly had no intention of retiring. I always had it in the back of my mind that someday I would come back into the cola business and revolutionize it my own way, but in the meantime I decided to go back into my old business of trying to help companies in trouble.

National Power & Light was one company that had gone into bankruptcy. It had tried to corner the utilities market, and the government, through the Securities and Exchange Commission, had forced it to liquidate. I saw this as the opportunity to acquire a company with assets and to use those assets for rebuilding other companies. I got permission from the SEC to buy control of National Power & Light on the condition that it would never go back into the utility business. That was fine by me, so I got together with a syndicate of investors who had confidence in what they thought I could do and bought control for a million dollars, which after liquidation meant that I would have National's $2 million in cash to play with. I renamed the company National Phoenix Industries and set out to do exactly what I had done twenty years before with the original Phoenix. Again, we would build companies up from the ashes of their own mismanagement.

The first company we bought was Nedick's Inc., an orange-drink and hot-dog stand chain with ninety outlets. Not only was it badly managed but its stores were pretty run-down. It was strictly mass catering for a fast turnover serving over 50 million quick meals a year with an average check of 21¢, but its profits for the year before, 1950, were just a little over $350,000. The first thing we did at Nedick's was to build up attendance. I put on special promotions and had a lucky-number contest once a week.

Everybody who came in to eat got a little slip with a number on it, and once a week we pulled out the numbers and the winner would get a mink coat or a trip to Florida or something. Attendance did go up, but my profit margin went down, and after about a year or so of this I figured out what the problem was. We were being robbed blind by our clerks. They would simply put the change in their pockets. For instance, somebody might have a check for 60¢ and the clerk would ring up 30¢ on the cash register and pocket the other 30¢. There was no way we could say that the change in their pockets belonged to us, because it was all in nickels, dimes, and quarters. No matter how much we built our business, we were still only operating at a $300,000 to $400,000 profit because of the sticky fingers of some of our staff.

All Nedick's employees belonged to a union, and I'd always made a habit in any company I went into of getting to know the union leader and trying to understand his problems so that he would understand mine. That's one of the reasons none of the companies I have been involved with ever had a union strike. The head of the union at Nedick's was a fellow by the name of Joseph McCarthy, and we got to be quite friendly. I knew his problem was that he had a terrific turnover in employees because they didn't get paid very much—as soon as they got a better job, they'd leave—and he understood my problem about the pilfering. We decided that the only way to stop it was to set some examples, so we put a couple of detectives into the stores and caught a few employees red-handed, but it was just a waste of time. The kids were poor, and the amount each one of them took was so small that the judges always let them loose.

Well, that was all certainly true, but it still meant that something like 30 percent of our profits was walking out the door every day, and there was no way we could make more than $300,000 to $400,000 a year. After about four years of this I decided the best thing to do was to let somebody else worry about it, so I sold it to ABC Vending Company. They're still running it, and they still haven't solved the problem—and they're still making a profit of around $300,000 to $400,000 a year, but they're content with that. I couldn't be. I wasn't willing to just sit there and not build. I've got to move ahead; I like to run. We made about a million dollars profit on the sale, but over four years that wasn't much to be thankful for, especially as we'd improved sales tremendously and improved the product. The orange drink was the best in town. We had a special roll made up that was better than anybody else's, and I wound up learning a great deal about how to make hot dogs— the best dog comes from the bull, not from the cow, because it takes the smoke much better—and the stores looked a lot better, so ABC Vending got a pretty good deal for their money. The only thing we were never able to improve at Nedick's was its profit.

Nedick's wasn't the only company in financial trouble because of bad management—the stock exchange was littered with their corpses—and one that interested me was Great American Industries. It was owned by the Pritzker family in Chicago and it consisted of two main companies: one called Rubatex which was based in Bedford, Virginia, and another with plants in Illinois that was one of the country's largest manufacturers of casters—big casters, little casters, casters of all sizes for every sort of domestic and industrial use imaginable. This second business was being run, more or less, by the Pritzkers' son, who was just a young kid having a good time. He had two airplanes, which he flew from one plant to another, both fully staffed with separate pilots, maintenance crews, and everything necessary to keep his toys operable—and toys they were, since they were totally unnecessary and they cost a mint. The first thing I did when I took over Great American Industries was to sell those two planes. The second thing I did was to ask young Pritzker to resign.

I've always maintained that it's a great mistake to bring family members into the business. It's been the downfall of too many businesses, because you can't fire your son, or daughter, or son-in-law, and you've got to run a business the way you play a game of football or basketball: You've got to play it to win, you can't just dribble along; and if you don't play to win, you've got to get the hell out of it. I don't believe people should be given soft jobs in a business just because they are related in some way or another, because you can't ever get rid of them without having an upheaval in the family.

My Uncle Harry had a daughter named Eleanor, and she went out and married a ne'er-do-well, a guy named Bert who wouldn't do anything but play around and drink. Well, Eleanor came to see her father one day and asked if he would take her husband into his business, and Uncle Harry said no, not under any conditions. But he would give him an allowance to live on and he would give it to him regularly as long as he didn't try to come into the business. That was just fine with Bert, because he was a nice fellow who didn't want to do a thing except sit through life. I remember one time when we were all up in the country together. Bert used to fish off the dock into the lake, and one day I came down to go canoeing and there he was sitting, smoking his pipe, with his line in the water, and I looked down and there was this fish hopping up and down. "Bert," I said, "you've got a fish on your line."

And he said: "I know. He's been there for half an hour. What's the hurry of pulling him up."

There he was, sitting in the sun, smoking away with a fish on the end of his line, and he was too lazy to pull the thing out. It wasn't going away, so what was the hurry. The damndest guy I ever knew. Nice fellow, Bert, but how right Uncle Harry was to give him an allowance to stay out of the business. It was much cheaper that way.

It was the same with Great American Industries: Get rid of the relatives and get rid of the deadwood. The caster manufacturing side of the business was too highly competitive to produce the profit margin I was interested in showing, so I sold off the factories in Illinois and concentrated on Rubatex, which began to show a great profit. Not long after that the union tried to come in and organize our factory in Virginia, and before long we were embroiled in a fight. Bedford was a small place, near Roanoke, and we practically controlled the town since we were by far the biggest thing in it. The townspeople wanted to see us grow and prosper, but they weren't very protective of the security of the plant, and while the union was picketing us, the police department was not very cooperative, so I thought it was a good time to teach the Bedford town officials a lesson.

For two months I paid all the workers in silver. I brought down armored trucks from Washington, D.C., filled with silver dollars and 50¢ pieces, and instead of paying out at the end of the week in $10 and $20 bills, everybody who worked at the plant got a big envelope filled with silver. Pretty soon the town was awash in silver coins, everybody from the butcher and baker to the shoemaker was handling nothing but silver. They all knew where this money came from, and as it became obvious that the entire economy of the town depended on our rubber plant their whole attitude changed. From there on out we had no further trouble.

I wasn't against the union per se—I've always been a union person myself and definitely pro-labor—and if they had unionized the plant it would have saved us money, because we were paying more than the union demanded. What I objected to was the way it dictated to its members. I knew that once they had unionized my employees and my plant, they would use that as a stepping stone to take on other plants. Almost all the laboring people I've ever worked with are decent, but when their leaders get a lust for power they can get so restrictive that they can shut down production at will.

By the mid-sixties Great American Industries, through Rubatex, was earning a profit of around $2 million a year—as opposed to the $500,000 or so when we took it over—and I used those profits to expand into some wholly owned subsidiaries like Great American Resources, which concentrated on natural resource ventures such as oil, gas, and copper searches and drillings, some of which paid off and some of which didn't.

In spite of success in all these fields, however, I was still itching to get back into the soft drink business, and when I thought the timing was right I again used some of the profits from Great American Industries to buy the American rights to an Irish firm called Cantrell & Cochrane, one of the oldest trademarks in the business. C & C had started out producing a tonic water that they exported to India, thus creating Indian Tonic. They were small, however, with only one plant, which was in Belfast, and this suited my needs perfectly. I wanted to test out my theories on canning and warehouse delivery, and with no franchises in my way, C & C would be my test pilot. I built a plant in New Jersey, got John Ritchie, one of my chemists from the old Pepsi days, to make up a good cola drink, and started selling C & C in cans. At first we sold in New Jersey, then came into New York two years later, in 1964, but it was an uphill struggle all the way. I simply couldn't get shelf space next to Pepsi and Coke, and since I was the only one putting out cola in cans, the public hadn't yet adjusted to it. Also, this was a time when the economy was riding high and the consumer wasn't all that impressed with the saving C & C offered them over the two major brands. I remember that one day I was down at the Morgan Guaranty bank and ran into an old friend of mine, Eugene Stetson, who was a vice-president on the board of Coca-Cola. "You know, Walter," he said, "you're making a great mistake trying to put soft drinks in cans. It'll never go. We've tested it down in Atlanta and it picks up the taste of the metal in the can. The public doesn't like it, and it'll never sell. We've decided that we'll never put Coca-Cola out except in a bottle, a *glass* bottle.

"Well, Eugene," I said, "that's your opinion, but they're doing it with beer, and it's going to come in soft drinks. But that's all up to you, I'm not running Coca-Cola."

Within a year they had to eat their own words, and the reason was that I had hit pay dirt with my cans of C & C by selling it to the military. At camps both here and abroad they had a terrible time with bottles and broken glass, and they loved the can; so when Coca-Cola saw little C & C suddenly getting big orders from the military, they swiftly changed their tune and got in on our business.

Nevertheless, the directors of Phoenix thought I was using a lot of money for a pet project, and they finally convinced me that I was indeed ahead of my time. C & C was making a profit of around $250,000 a year, but what was that next to the $2 million or so our other ventures were doing? So I sold the company to John Ritchie and the employees at the New Jersey plant. They carried it on, and although it remained primarily in the New York metropolitan area, it did very well. So I knew my experiment and my ideas were right.

19

Jefferson Island, a little island in the bay right off
Annapolis, Maryland, was bought by a group of rich
Democrats who formed the Jefferson Island Club as a
place where they could all get together and relax away
from the pressures of Washington. Its members were
the most influential Democrats in the government, and
any Democratic President of the United States was
automatically president of the club. I was a member
of the Jefferson Island Club, their token Republican,
and would go down there regularly for duck shooting,
fishing, and just generally lazing about. That's where I
first really got to know Franklin Roosevelt, one of the
finest men we've ever had in government, and Harry

Truman, one of the straightest. While Truman was President I was a member of the club's board of governors, and we would sit around to all hours of the night playing poker. There were about seven of us in the game, six Democrats and me, and they'd always says, "Let's get the damn Republican's money." I knew they were kidding, but at the same time I never wanted to win too much money from them.

It was difficult for me to walk a tightrope with Harry Truman, but we always got on very well together—even if he did call me "that goddamn Republican"—and he knew he could depend on me for almost anything, provided it wasn't political. Just because we represented different parties didn't mean we weren't working towards the same goals. One day he asked me to come down to Washington to see if I could find out what he could possibly do to help Haiti. The country was in very bad shape financially because they didn't have any exports. They needed money, but Truman didn't want to give them money; he wanted to know what he could do to put the people to work. "Walter," he said, "I want to form a commission to study the economic situation in Haiti, and I want you to be chairman of that commission. Will you go down there for me, study the island, and come back with a report that tells me what you think we can do to give them some business that will put them to work?"

Nobody said no to Harry Truman, so I flew down with Ruth, and the two of us lived in this little place way up in the hills, the damndest place I ever saw. The president of Haiti was named Paul Magloíre—this was before Papa Doc Duvalier became dictator—and he was going to be our personal guide, or more to the point he was Ruth's personal guide while I got the chief of police. We spent about a month and a half down there and went over every part of the island with them and with various local representatives who would show up wherever we went to plead their special case. It was one of the most beautiful countries I had ever seen, but at the same time the most pathetic in the world, because the people were starving and there was absolutely nothing for them to do. However, it seemed to me that there were two things that could offer possible employment: One was to raise sisal in the middle of the island for rope and twine, and the other was to put up a soap factory to use their coconuts to make coconut soap, which was very much in demand.

I met with President Magloíre and told him I thought we could get some industry going down there provided he would pass some laws to give outside industries twenty years without import/export taxes, laws that would stand up in his legislature and that couldn't be canceled. Latin American governments have a great way of getting you in there and after you've built your plants and created your industry, passing exorbitant tax laws, knocking you silly with licencing fees, and then prohibiting any currency export or money exchange, so that it all disappears down the hole and into the pockets of corrupt officials. I was determined that this not happen with any future U.S. investment, and I needed the president's assurance.

Magloíre readily agreed, and I returned to Washington and made my report to Truman, making it clear that I thought nothing should be done unless we received the legal guarantees in advance. Of course, the laws were never passed and nothing was ever done. Truman never gave them any money, because he knew it would go right into Magloíre's pocket or to some of his cronies, so Haiti is in the same shape today that it was thirty years ago. Basically the entire country was just like a sick industry being ruined by poor management, but like any industry I went into to rebuild, I needed control first. Haiti refused to hand over that control in the form of legal tax and currency guarantees, so there was no way we were going to go in there and get soaked. In industry you can get rid of dishonest and incompetent management, but in countries like Haiti pilferage from the top is a way of life, or—for most of the starving population below—a way of death.

A few years ago I was in the Philippines and one of the big industrialists I had known from my Pepsi days invited me out to his country house for Sunday lunch. I drove out from Manila through the countryside to their place, which was the last word in luxury. It was a vast estate completely surrounded by fencing and barbed wire, with fierce dogs all over the place reined in by guards who carried shotguns and machine guns and slept with the dogs on the grounds. It didn't leave me with a comfortable feeling at all, but it didn't seem to bother anybody except me. My host had invited a large number of other influential businessmen to lunch, and everybody seemed to take the contrast between great, ostentatious wealth and grinding poverty as the normal way of life, which, of course, in the Philippines and so many parts of the world today it is—so much so that nobody noticed it but the visiting "ugly American."

During lunch my host told me he was putting out a new line of paper manufactured from the wood pulp that was a surplus in the Philippines, and I remarked that if it was of good quality he certainly wouldn't have any trouble selling it in the U.S. "Perhaps not," he said. "We don't have any trouble in South and Central America, because we know what the price is, we know who to pay in the government, what the correct bribe is, and we get what we want, but the trouble with you in the United States is that you can't do that. You can never know for certain because your country has different, very curious standards."

To a certain extent, what my host was saying was quite true. Throughout most of the world, bribery is the *only* thing that works efficiently. It's simply part of the price. It's the norm throughout most of Asia, South and Central America, and around the Mediterranean. I've personally encountered it, and I've had to deal with it, and it always turns my stomach. If I wanted something done in Mexico, I'd be told what it would cost and who to pay, and of course I would have to pay it. But in America, and indeed in much of Northern Europe, it is the exception rather than the rule, and although it's an exception I've seen practiced in politics and business since I first opened my eyes to both some sixty years ago, it is something that in this country I can spit on and grind into the dirt where it belongs. We have our problems, but we seem to work them out as decent human beings, which is one of the reasons I have always been proud to be that "ugly American."

There is a long tradition in this country of public service, of civic duty, not for personal gain or aggrandizement, but for the common good. I am on the board of Temple Emanu-El not only because I just happen to be a Jew, since I've never been religious one way or another, nor have I ever been exposed to any personal prejudice, but because it is my community and I can help in a professional capacity. I went through Harvard, the Navy, and my early years seeing blacks primarily as entertainers, athletes, or laborers, yet once my consciousness was awakened, once I was made aware of my own blindness, I worked to correct society's blindspots through my work with the unions and the scholarships at Pepsi, and on the anti-discrimination councils in the state of New York.

Again, let an old man add that this is not a self-congratulatory pat on the back; it is just the way I believe things should be. We grow, we learn, and we use what we have learned through growth to help our fellow man. I, for one, was never interested in living behind a barbed-wire fence surrounded by guard dogs. If that had been the choice, I'd be on the other side of the fence ready to rip it apart along with the society that put me there.

But of all the people I have ever known who sincerely liked people and wanted to be in public service, there was no one to touch Nelson Rockefeller. He was the most outstanding servant to the public I've ever known. Nelson and I grew up together in politics as liberal Republicans, and while we both may have made mistakes along the way—and he had a far greater opportunity to make those mistakes than almost anyone—we trusted each other, so when he was publicly humiliated at the Republican National Convention in 1964, it was enough to make me break ranks publicly with the party that had been a major part of my life for over forty years.

The sixties seem a long time away even now, but lest we forget, they were tumultuous years—revolutionary years in many ways. When the Republican convention opened in San Francisco in 1964 there were two leading contenders for the presidential nomination, Nelson Rockefeller and Barry Goldwater, but when Rockefeller came up for nomination, the Goldwater gang wouldn't even give him a chance to talk. They shouted him down and steamrolled the Goldwater nomination, leaving Nelson out in the elegant cold. We've always had a lot of extreme factions in American politics, and it's fine to let them hoot and holler, but this was different. This was a bunch of ultra-ultra-conservatives who had managed to get hold of the machinery of a major party, my party. I had to do something.

I knew Goldwater, and he was a very funny fellow. His brain and his mouth didn't seem to work together. He'd say the goddamndest things, which he didn't really mean. You couldn't count on him. It got so bad with him that when he was campaigning across the country by plane, nobody was allowed to talk to him— not just the press, but other politicians—because he'd say things that were completely wrong and that he really didn't mean even at the time. It got to the point that if somebody wanted to ask a question they had to put it in writing. It then went up to a committee who took it to Goldwater. Together they figured out an answer—something more or less sensible—and that's what went back to the questioner. People simply weren't allowed to talk to him, because nobody knew what the hell he was going to say. He was my party's candidate, so I knew it was time to organize.

I formed the Independent Republicans and Citizens for Johnson, not so much to get Lyndon Johnson re-elected as to make sure that Goldwater didn't get near the White House. I started it out with $15,000 of my own money and sent out letters on my own stationery. Pretty soon the cash started rolling in—and from the most unexpected sources—and before long we were organized in forty-six states. There was a great secret swing among Republicans, especially those who were state leaders and didn't want to see their states go down in flames with Goldwater but who at the same time were afraid to show their true colors. They wanted me to go in and pull their candidates out of the mud, and I found myself going all over the U.S. helping local Republicans under my label, Independent Republicans and Citizens for Johnson.

As a result we elected a lot of local candidates under our banner who otherwise would have been defeated, and of course Goldwater lost the presidential election by the largest popular majority in U.S. history. Johnson got 61 percent of the popular vote and 486 electoral votes, while Goldwater managed only 38 percent of the vote and 52 electoral votes. The President seemed very grateful, but then I really didn't do it for him. I did it to stop the Goldwater gang, who I felt were the greatest threat to this country in our time—and to help Nelson Rockefeller.

During my campaign for Johnson my relations with Pepsi-Cola became, through an odd set of circumstances, even more strained. Back when I was first starting up Pepsi, Admiral McDonald, who at the time was a senior partner of Hornblower & Weeks, a big brokerage house that owned a lot of Pepsi-Cola stock, came in to see me and praised the company highly, saying he thought it was really going to go places. Then he added that he had a son-in-law who was out of a job and asked if I would give him a chance at Pepsi. I told him how I felt about giving somebody a job just because he happened to be well connected through family, but I was willing to try anything or anybody, so I asked him to come in for a talk. The guy's name was Don Kendall, and he was a personable enough young fellow, so I hired him as a syrup salesman in the New York area for $25 a week. He did such a good job that by 1964 he was the president of the company.

When the news came out that I was forming Independent Republicans and Citizens for Johnson, all the newspapers had "Walter Mack, former president of Pepsi-Cola," but of course nobody ever bothered to read the "former" part. The story was hot, and before the ink was even dry on the evening edition of the papers I got a call from Milwood W. Martin, better known as Pidge, who was head of Pepsi's legal department. He said that the company's switchboard was lighting up like the Fourth of July with callers wanting to know what was going on, because Don Kendall was a very close friend of Nixon's and it was all getting very embarrassing. "Well, Pidge," I said, "what am I supposed to do about that? I've done everything I can. Whenever anybody asks me, I tell them I'm the *former* president and no longer associated with Pepsi. What else can I do?"

"Well, it's very delicate," said Pidge, "and you've got to do something because we're in a terrible position."

"Well, to hell with you," I said. "So is the country." And I hung up.

Kendall remained a great friend of Nixon's right through. When Nixon was out of office he hired his firm as Pepsi-Cola's lawyers, and in fact Nixon himself was

Pepsi's general lawyer. This meant that a percentage of the large fees Pepsi paid the firm went to Nixon as a partner but more important was the fact that a good portion of his traveling expenses were paid directly by Pepsi. And he traveled the world over, so it might be said that when he finally became President, Pepsi was largely responsible for his being knowledgeable about world affairs.

As a matter of fact, John Mitchell, who later became our controversial attorney general, was Nixon's partner in the law firm and did all the work. Nixon was just a figurehead, although he got all the fees from Pepsi and this allowed him to live and travel well. Once he got into office it was very simple for him to pay off his obligations to Pepsi and Kendall by helping them get into Russia. A deal was made whereby the Russians would pay for the Pepsi concentrate with vodka, Stolíchnaya, which Pepsi then sold in this country, and that's how they got their money out. It was no coincidence that Pepsi moved into Russia while Nixon was in the White House, any more than it *just so happened* that Coca-Cola made their deal with China while a Georgian was President. Chickens do come home to roost after all.

20

I've been in a great many businesses in my life, and the soft drink business is still, to me, the most fascinating there is. There is just nothing like it anywhere, for a number of reasons: It's not seasonal, and it doesn't change in style; your product is good year in and year out. It's a cash business, which eliminates accounts receivable, and your inventory is always good. There are no seconds; your shelf life is indefinite, so there's no spoilage; and the return on capital investment is out of this world. There's not another business in which you have no receivables, no worry about inventory, no worry about spoilage or shelf life, and with such an enormous turnover you can make a return on your investment of 1000 percent a year. Take a bottler whose plant and machinery cost him in the neighborhood of a million dollars. With any luck at all he's probably making $5 million profit every year, so he's getting his money back five times over from now until doomsday. It's a sweetheart business, and I was anxious to get back into it.

In addition, I am a great guy for liking the masses. They're my people, I was brought up with them, I know them, I like them, and I appreciate their judgment. I always wanted to cater to the mass purchasing power of this country, and there isn't anything that does that like a soft drink. Fifteen years ago the total liquid consumption in the United States was 182 gallons per person, with soft drinks accounting for about 18 gallons of that. Today the total consumption remains about the same, but soft drinks now account for almost 39 gallons of that total, already passing fruit juice and milk and about to overtake per capita consumption of tap water.

Cola drinks account for almost 65 percent of the entire soft drink business, well ahead of their nearest rival, the lemon and lime drink at 12 percent, while root beer and orange drinks are at around 5 percent each, and ginger ale a little less at 4. These percentages are firm. You can knock your head off spending millions on advertising and you won't budge them. The reason is that there is a certain proportion of the population that likes a lemon and lime drink, a certain proportion that prefers orange, and so on, and that just can't be changed. A few years ago Hires Root Beer came out with a $10 million advertising campaign, and that year their sales went up from 5 to 5¼ percent. $10 million for a quarter of a percent. It was a waste of money. When Philip Morris bought Seven-Up in 1978 for $125 million they doubled their ad budget and tried to push their third-ranking product—after Coke and Pepsi—into a new market. The head of Philip Morris's beer and soda division talked to me one day and asked me what I thought their chances were. "It's very simple," I said to him. "The people who like a lemon and lime drink such as Seven-Up will continue buying your product, but you can spend $100 million in advertising and you're not going to make any appreciable dent in those percentages." Still, they went ahead and spent $40 million in advertising, and the net result was that Seven-Up's share of the market dropped from 5.9 to 5.6 percent.

The reason this country drinks so much cola is not because of the money spent on advertising, but because of the drink itself. The secret is in that little cola nut and the properties it has to make you feel good. Everything else is just another refreshing drink, but a properly made cola drink does give you a lift no other drink can. There are over three hundred cola brands on the market, but few companies know how to make it. As a result, most of them are just so much bellywash, which is why Coke and Pepsi between them account for 70 percent of that lucrative cola market. That was the market I wanted to tap, and I certainly should know how to do it by now.

I've always had the name King-Cola in the back of my mind. If you were to name a drink today—or a soap or a grocery product—you wouldn't call it Pepsi-Cola or Coca-Cola. Those names have become great because so much money was spent promoting them for so long, but today you would name your product Tab, or Whiz, or Frostie, or something like that, and King-Cola seemed to me to have the right ring; so long before I was even ready to start up the company, I registered the name and waited my turn.

When I saw that C & C was taking off by using my marketing techniques I knew that it was time to get out of Great American Industries and back into soft drinks, but still I had to wait until I could get together with Tommy Elmezzi. He was my chief chemist at Pepsi, the man who had created Pepsi-Cola, and I wanted him to formulate a new, improved cola drink for the eighties. But he couldn't even start experimenting until 1978, when his negative contract finally ran out with Pepsi and he would be free to get back into the cola business. Once he was ready to go I put together a group of experienced Coca-Cola and Pepsi-Cola people and together we formed King-Cola. Ben Domont, a former Pepsi bottler from Indianapolis who had sold his franchise to Borden, the dairy people, for $25 million, came in and helped organize; John Donlevy, who had run all the Pepsi plants and was responsible for 25 percent of their total U.S. sales, became our president; Dick Harvey, who had been executive vice-president of Coca-Cola for thirty-five years, came in on a consulting basis; and I kicked myself upstairs to be chairman of the board. Right down the line, we started out with the top people.

When I first formed Pepsi I made the big mistake of not looking far enough into the future, and as a result I saddled myself with far too many franchises and too many middlemen. I decided that in forming this company I would look way ahead and form it in such a way that no matter what happened in the U.S. we would be prepared to take advantage of it. So instead of the hundreds of small franchises that Coke and Pepsi are still stuck with, I divided the country into twenty-nine huge areas, which I call kingdoms. Those territories are so big that they give mass purchasing power to the people who form them, ensuring that they will be able to produce under any conditions and no matter what laws the government may pass. And at last my system of delivering directly to supermarket warehouses could become a reality.

To start a new cola drink against the entrenched Coke and Pepsi, even with a lower basic cost and a streamlined approach, is generally considered a dangerous undertaking, and many have been tempted but turned away. However, there is a construction job to be done—to modernize the cola industry, to eliminate the old-fashioned, costly, franchised small territories system and pass the savings and lower costs on to the public. King-Cola will have its ups and downs before it breaks through, but eventually its new way of operating will prevail, and it should have an important place in the cola industry.

Who ever said that eighty-three was too old to start a new company?

When you go into a business, any business, you have to go all the way—as the saying goes, you can't be a little bit pregnant—and just because I'm starting up anew at my advanced age doesn't mean I'm playing at it. That's not something I could ever do. I have to go all the way or get out and go another way, and the older I get, the more important this becomes; because even though my luck may not be running out, my time is, and there's still a hell of a lot I want to do.

Most of my classmates from Harvard, and even those who graduated twenty years after me, retired a long time ago, and they're all bored to death. They don't know what to do with themselves. They get up in the morning just to sit around, and to get out of their house they go down to the Harvard Club to play some backgammon or bridge, and they drink entirely too much. Then they might go over to their broker's office to watch the tape go by while they drink some more, and finally they go home and listen to their arteries get hard. They don't last very long, because they have no particular interest; but, of course, they all think I'm nuts. They think I ought to go out to graze like some old used-up horse, but the funny thing is, I don't feel much like an old used-up horse, and I'm not all that fond of grazing.

Not too long ago I had lunch with the treasurer of Continental Can. We've been good friends for years, so we speak freely with one another, and during lunch he said: "Walter, I've often wondered what makes you tick. I just don't understand it. I'm going to be sixty-five in about six months and I can't wait to retire."

"That's great," I said, "but what the hell are you going to do with yourself?"

"Well, I don't know what I *am* going to do, but I can't wait just to be able to sit back and not have to get up at seven every morning and rush to the office."

"That's fine," I added, "but try it for a while first. Take my advice: Before you do it, stay home and listen to the soap operas and watch the game shows that fill up so many other people's lives, and then decide what you're going to do with the rest of your day—and the days after that. Take about two or three months of that before you decide to retire completely. It may even work for you, but at least you'll know one way or the other beforehand."

A lot of older people look at retirement as a sort of prolonged vacation, but I've found that most of my friends who take off on a long vacation late in life come back much more worse for wear than they went out. They eat too much, drink too much, and change their entire pace too quickly, and the body and mind don't know how to adjust. All too often it ends up in a heart attack. There's no way I could take off a month now and just do nothing, because there's always something to do. If I weren't traveling, seeing new places and meeting new people, I'd go up to my place in Connecticut, and there's always a lot to do around there. If I'm not spraying the trees or digging up the vegetable garden, I get involved with a new project that keeps me going. I couldn't just take off three weeks to go fishing or go down to Palm Beach and do the whole social scene. But then, maybe that's because I did a lot of that in my younger days so I know what it's all about, and I know that it doesn't hold any attraction for me. My life has been one long vacation, in a way, since my work and my involvement are my relaxation, so any sort of retirement as prolonged vacation would finish me off.

I firmly believe that we are put on earth to do things, and I think that you are much happier and get along better with your fellow man if you're doing something constructive. My birth certificate tells me I should have disappeared a long time ago, and although I've never made as much money for myself as I have for others, I certainly never need to work another day in my life.

Each person has to figure out what's best for himself, but the best thing for all of us is to keep doing, keep going. It might be in commerce or it might be in charity, or even a combination of the two, but it should be constructive labor. We are never too old to contribute something. Although politics no longer holds the fascination for me that it once did, business still does, and one of the truly great pleasures I have is in helping other people, giving a guy a job so that he can build himself up.

I've had a longer and more profitable life than most —that, I'll be the first to admit—and because I've always tried to heed the advice that my old sea captain passed on to me some sixty years ago, I haven't missed too many opportunities, and I have no regrets. I've never had a bad experience—narrow escapes, yes; difficulties, yes; but never a bad taste—and if I had to go back and do it over again I would do exactly the same thing. I don't know how other people live or what they did or didn't do with their lives, I only know about my own. I only know what I did, and as far as I'm concerned I've lived a very mellow, full life, an understanding life.

Most people in this country don't realize that we are entering a new world; a combination of Wendell Willkie's "one world" and a new world typified and brought about by the hopeless plight of the *colonas* in Cuba.

Human beings can't live for too long without hope of improving their lot and that of their children. Given the example and the opportunity, they will rise up—

and even be willing to die to break the hopeless enslavement they have been in. That was what happened in Cuba, that is what is now happening in much of Eastern Europe, and that is what has happened in most of the poorer undeveloped countries around the world. The peons, the *colonas,* the peasants—call them what you will—will not now work for the pittance, the starvation wage they have been limited to. They are demanding better conditions and hope for a better life for themselves and their children.

If you observe it closely, you can see and feel it happening. The people will not cut sugarcane in Cuba for what they received when I started our plantation there forty years ago; the result is high sugar prices. The peasants of Brazil won't gather the coffee beans for the low pay they formerly received; we are paying much higher coffee prices today than three years ago. The same is true for rubber from Malaysia, bauxite for aluminum from Jamaica, tin from Bolivia, and so on down the line.

What most people are calling inflation today I see on a much broader scale as the start of a new world— the readjustment and growth period before moving to a higher plateau—the awakening of the depressed poorer people who are demanding their right to hope and the opportunity to work to improve their lot.

We are moving into one world—in the end, a new and better one for all. I am delighted to have been, and will continue to be, a part of that new and better world. Not only the growth and development of stagnant businesses, but now the growth and development of stagnant countries and their people, is something that all Americans should welcome and be a part of.

For all of us, "Full speed ahead!" Even though we will go through troubled waters for a while, we have what it takes to lead the way through this adjustment period, and I will continue to do what I can to help.